ABOUT THE AUTHOR

Raghu Palat is one of India's leading writers on finance, taxation and banking. Apart from writing regularly on these subjects for financial newspapers and magazines, he frequently lectures on finance and banking to professional bodies. What sets his writings apart from other writers of finance is the lucid way in which he explains a very difficult subject. He is the author of four other extremely popular books—"The Magic of Ratios", "The Credit Report", "Tax Planning for the Salaried Employee" and "Jaico's Wonderworld of Investments" (all published by JAICO).

A great grandson of His Highness the late Sir Rama Varma, Maharaja of Cochin and the late Sir Chettur Sankaran Nair (a member of the Viceroy's Privy Council and a former President of the Indian National Congress), Mr. Palat was educated at some of the most prestigious educational institutions in the country—The Lawrence School at Lovedale and The Madras Christian College at Tambaram. He is a Fellow of the Institute of Chartered Accountants in England and Wales and an Associate of the Institute of Chartered Accountants of India.

Other Books By The Same Author

- The Credit Report
- Understanding Financial Ratios in Business
- Tax Planning For The Salaried Employees
- A Complete Guide For The NRI
- Interview Tips

How to Read
ANNUAL REPORTS
&
BALANCE SHEETS

Raghu Palat

JAICO PUBLISHING HOUSE
Mumbai • Delhi • Bangalore • Kolkata
Hyderabad • Chennai • Ahmedabad • Bhopal

Published by Jaico Publishing House
121 Mahatma Gandhi Road
Mumbai - 400 023
jaicopub@vsnl.com
www.jaicobooks.com

© Raghu Palat

HOW TO READ ANNUAL REPORTS & BALANCE SHEETS
ISBN 81-7224-101-1

Ninth Jaico Impression: 2006

Printed by
Uday Offset
Kewal Industrial Estate, Gala No.104, Ist Floor
Senapati Bapat Marg, Lower Parel, Mumbai-13.

This book is dedicated to my elder daughter

Divya Nishima Malini Palat

Who is a constant delight

PREFACE

Companies are evaluated, investment decisions are made and funds are committed on the basis of opinions arrived at on scrutinising the Annual Report and the Financial Statements of a company. Deals are clinched and arguments are won on quoting information read and figures procured from the Annual Report and yet, there is a lack of knowledge of financial statements—an ignorance of the innovativeness of creative accounting and the manipulations of accounting principles. There is a lack of understanding of a Balance Sheet and a Profit and Loss Account and on how to analyse these statements.

The purpose of this book is to introduce the reader to the Annual Report and to make the reader aware of what to expect and to teach him how to read it intelligently.

The reader will be initially introduced to the components in an Annual Report, namely, The Directors' Report, The Audit Report and The Financial Statements, and would be made aware of:
(a) what goes into them
(b) what they look like
(c) what the terms mean
(d) what is included in the terms mentioned above
(e) what to look for.

It is then proposed to introduce the reader to ratio analysis and the analysis of the financial statements in order to enable him to evaluate the strengths and determine the weaknesses of companies and to educate him on how accounting principles can be manipulated. Finally other factors that determine the market price of a share, the success of a company and external factors that can influence the performance of a company are discussed.

The importance of this knowledge can never be understated. Armed with the information and knowledge contained in this book, the investor, the owner of shares in a company or anyone interested in knowing the performance of a company by reading an Annual Report will be far better equipped to arrive at a balanced conclusion.

This book on how to read and analyse an Annual Report is not meant for professional accountants or finance executives, although I daresay they would find it useful, but for the uninitiated —the businessman, the student, the non-financial executive, the investor, the housewife and anyone else who at anytime purchases shares, owns shares or wishes to read intelligently the Annual Report of a company.

It is my hope that this book would help the reader to unravel the mysteries of the Financial Statements and comprehend the innovativeness of creative accounting. Above all it should make him read an Annual Report analytically aware of what to look for, where and what the various terms mean. In short the reader should finally be able to read between and beyond the lines.

I have to thank several individuals who helped in different ways and had it not been for them this book would not have seen the light of day. I thank Neil Weiss and Leo Bernstein of New York University who taught me on what to really look at in an Annual Report. I thank the editors of Business World, The Independent, The Sunday Observer and Fortune India for their encouragement and for their publishing the articles I write for their publications. I thank Mr. Ashwin Shah and Mr. Sharma of Jaico Publishing House for their support and their trust. And finally I thank my family—my wife Pushpa and my two daughters Divya and Nikhila for their love, their encouragement and their faith in my ability.

CONTENTS

CONTENTS

BRILOFF'S LAW

Whenever ants swarm, the pot will not only
contain a bit of money, but will also be
filled with accounting gimmicks.

Abraham J. Briloff in "Unaccountable Accounting"

INTRODUCTION

The Annual Report

Companies compete with each other to present impressive Annual Reports to their shareholders, lenders and potential investors. Prizes are awarded by august bodies such as the Institute of Chartered Accountants for the report that is, in their opinion, the best presented. A lot of work goes into the preparation of the Annual Report. Multi-coloured pie and bar charts are included to illustrate and explain to the shareholders facts such as the growth of the company and the manner in which the revenue earned has been utilised. There are pictures of the newly painted factory; of new machines acquired; of the Chairman at his desk looking forbidding yet wise and of the Board of Directors, the directors individually attempting to appear professional, capable and yet benevolent. As a consequence Annual Reports tend to be bulky.

The average shareholder does not look much further. If the Annual Report appears worthy of the company whose name it bears, if the photographs are impressive and the company has paid a reasonable dividend, the shareholder reads no more. He sits back content in the belief that the fortunes of the company are in good hands.

This must not be the criteria by which a company is judged. Rather than be convinced on the state of the affairs of a company by gazing at charts and impressive arrays of figures and statistics, the reader of the report, whether he be investor or shareholder or creditor or just another interested person would be wise to delve deeper—to read between and beyond the lines and to peep behind the figures.

The purpose of this book is to guide the reader through the Annual Report, to explain the financial statements prepared and to make him aware of the innovativeness of creative accounting and the ambiguities that can arise by the manipulation of accounting principles.

PART I

PART I

1

THE DIRECTORS' REPORT

The first report that a shareholder or reader of the annual statements of a company is confronted with is the directors' report.

The directors report is a summation of the activities of the company in the period reported on—its results, its sales, its divisions and other relevant factors including of course the dividends that are recommended to be paid to the shareholders.

All directors' reports are well written. Every sentence, nay every word has been subjected to the most piercing scrutiny. Every happening of beneficial importance is catalogued and mentioned in a way that would make appear to the casual reader that the company is in good hands. And to an extent this is really what the directors' report attempts to do—it attempts more often than not to give to the shareholders a feeling that the directors are worthy of the trust reposed and the responsibility vested in them by the shareholders. In many cases they are but there is a tendency to gloss over unhappy situations at times or not to mention them at all.

In order therefore to become aware of all the facts it is necessary to read beyond the lines. The "blowing of one's trumpet" by the directors must not be taken at its face value.

The directors' report of Reliance Industries Ltd. for the year ended December 31, 1986 shows under its financial results (see Exhibit 1) a gross profit before interest and depreciation of Rs. 129.39 crores. As the expense of interest and depreciation has not been deducted it is difficult to actually determine whether the results were better than the previous year. This is attempted in Exhibit II. On restating the profit and loss account, it is immediately apparent that:
  (i) the results of the company have indeed not been good as against a trading profit of Rs. 53.21 crores in 1985. The company has in 1986 made a profit of only Rs. 14.16 crores.

5

(ii) The dividend for the year has actually been made from the profits of previous years. The balance brought forward has depleted by Rs. 13.6 crores. The capital of the company has thus decreased.

(iii) As a consequence of lower profitability even the transfer to general reserve is from the previous years profits (partially). This is arrived at as follows:

	(Rs. in crores)
Decrease in balance brought forward (14.52-1.92)	13.60
Accounted for by	
Dividend on equity shares	12.90
Transfer to general reserves (partial)	0.70
	13.60

Exhibit I

	(Rs. in crores)	
	1986	1985
Gross profit before interest and depreciation	129.39	133.25
Add : (a) Surplus balance brought forward from previous year	14.52	14.91
(b) Investment allowance (utilised) reserve written back	25.00	—
Less: Provisions and/or appropriations		
(a) Interest	54.24	24.45
(b) Depreciation	60.98	37.46
(c) Investment allowance reserve	36.00	22.80
(d) Taxation reserve	—	10.00
(e) Differential dividend pertaining to previous year	—	0.05
(f) Net effect of reversal of interest capitalised	—	8.13
(g) Recommended dividend		
(i) on 11% cumulative redeemable preference shares	0.03	0.03
(ii) On 15% cumulative redeemable preference shares	0.83	0.83
(iii) On equity shares	12.90	24.89
(h) Transferred to general reserve	2.00	5.00
Balance carried to balance sheet	1.92	14.52

Exhibit II

	(Rs. in crores)	
	1986	1985
Gross profit before interest and depreciation	129.39	133.25
Less: Interest	54.25	24.45
Depreciation	60.98	37.46
Profit after interest and taxation	14.16	71.34
Less: Taxation reserve	—	10.00
Profit after tax	14.16	61.34
Less: Prior year adjustment	—	8.13
Net effect of reversal of interest capitalised	14.16	53.21
Less: Appropriation of profit prior to dividends investment allowance (Net)	11.00	22.80
Profit (loss) after initial appropriations	3.16	30.41
Less: Dividends and reserves		
Differential dividend of previous year	—	0.05
On 11% preference shares	0.03	0.03
On 15% preference shares	0.83	0.83
On equity shares	12.90	24.89
Transferred to general reserve	2.00	5.00
Net profit (loss) after appropriations	(12.60)	(0.39)
Balance brought forward	14.52	14.91
Balance carried forward	1.92	14.52

The auditors report draws attention to two notes to the accounts which have a very telling effect on the results.

(a) Note 13 states the company has changed its method of accounting for the disposal of waste generated. If the company had been consistent in the manner this had been accounted the profit would have been lower by Rs. 11.72 crores.

(b) It is stated in Note 14 that the company had changed its method of valuation of inventories. The profits would have been higher in 1986 by Rs. 5.10 crores had the company been consistent.

The net effect of the change of accounting principles is that the company has increased its profits by Rs. 6.62 crores. The true operating profit in 1986 under consistent accounting practices would have been Rs. 7.50 and not Rs. 14.16. This is quite a difference.

The directors' report of Star Industrial and Textile Enterprises Ltd. for the year December 31, 1985 states "with reference to the observations made by the auditors in the report, the notes on accounts are self-explanatory and therefore do not call for any further comments under Section 217(3) of the Companies Act 1956." This paragraph does not really attract attention. Nothing is explained and it appears to be a standard requirement of the directors' report.

On probing further, the points made by the auditors is far from casual and are in fact very important. They state, among others.

1. There is a demand by excise authorities of Rs. 39,68,802.
2. Customs duty under dispute amounts to Rs. 3,44,500.
3. There is arrears of fixed cumulative preference dividend of Rs. 4,72,824.
4. Leave arrears and wages of Rs. 14,38,123 has not been provided for.
5. Non provision for the depletion in value of investments amounting to Rs. 12,40,000, doubtful debts of Rs. 44,40,037 and interest of Rs. 26,27,212.
6. Non payment of Rs. 70,03,358 in respect of provident fund, employees state insurance, tax deducted at source and other government dues.

The directors' report also gives the reader a valuable insight to the activities of the business.

It is stated in the directors' report of Hindustan Lever Ltd. for 1986 "sales volumes of the company's products continued to grow in response to sustained consumer demand. Lifebuoy, the common man's toilet soap, continues to lead the toilet soap market in the country and scales new heights. Satisfactory progress was also registered with Lux toilet soap which was relaunched in early 1986. Particularly heartening was the substantial increase in sales registered by the two premium detergent products, Surf and Rin."

3

"Production of cement rose from 5.40 lac tonnes to 6 lac tonnes, thus achieving 110% capacity utilisation", says Indian Rayon's director's report for 1986-87. "This satisfactory performance was recorded despite a 70% power cut imposed in Karnataka throughout the period under review. The excellent market reputation and better quality of cement produced here, enabled a higher price realisation. These two factors—higher capacity utilisation and higher price realisation—together enabled the division to successfully withstand the pressures generated by the rise in input costs, including those of coal, power, railway freight and royalty on limestone and thus maintain profitability".

A paragraph such as the one described above does inform the reader the difficulties the division faced, the problems that had to be grappled with and the result. Often however, there is a tendency to mention at length details of successes and not dwell in regard to areas where difficulties were experienced so that the reader is not really sure after reading the statement what actually is happening.

In Indian Rayon's 1986-87 report it is also stated in regard to Midnapur Cotton Mills that "although there was improvement in production efficiency, the working results were not satisfactory because of the increase in production costs and lower sales realisation".

A statement such as this leaves the reader no wiser than before. In fact it actually makes him wonder what actually is happening. More often than not, the mills must have made losses and the company is striving hard to turn it around without too much success.

A directors' report informs the reader of new projects and the direction the company proposes to take.

Vam Organic Chemicals directors' report speaks of new projects. "India Glycols, promoted by your company to manufacture 20,000 MT of monoethylene glycol (MEG) at a project cost of Rs. 80.25 crores is making rapid progress..... The collaborators are Scientific Design inc. of U.S.A. whose process accounts for the largest installed capacity of MEG in the world..... A number of other projects are also being considered and we believe, that your company will soon enter into a rapid growth phase."

The directors' report of Reliance (1986) details a number of new projects that it is in the process of implementation. Among these is a Petro chemical process and it plans to diversify into electronics. "Your company has decided to enter the rapidly growing field of plastic resins, and has obtained a letter of intent for the manufacture of 50,000 tonnes of high density polyethylene (HDPL) and 1,00,000 tonnes of poly vinyl chloride (PVC) per annum..... Your company has received a clearance from the government to manufacture 15,00,000 colour glass shells and 5,00,000 colour picture tubes annually involving a capital outlay of over Rs. 200 crores. Diversification in this field by the company is yet another project in the series of projects of import substitution taken up by the company to reduce dependence on imported items by the country."

The directors' report thus gives a reader an idea of the diversification plans a company has. A reader, knowing or considering industry conditions, can determine whether this diversification or new project could be wise. A diversification in recent times that was a near disaster was Burrough Wellcome's diversification to sports goods—Nike Sportswear in particular. The point that is being made is that although companies must diversify to spread the risks of industrial slumps all diversifications may not suit a company. The reader must evaluate for himself.

Finance is also discussed in detail in Directors' report, especially the raising of finance. Indian Rayon's 1986-87 directors' report states:. "During the year under review the company issued convertible debentures of Rs. 68.70 crores on a right basis to the equity shareholders. Additionally, convertible debentures of Rs. 5 crores were issued to non-resident Indians. The debentures issue received an excellent response. Your company retained the 25% excess subscription and refunded the balance. The non convertible debenture issue of Rs. 80 crores was also fully subscribed."

It was stated in Larsen and Toubro, 1985-86 directors' report

"Against the term loans aggregating Rs. 36.80 crores sanctioned by the financial institutions/banks for expansion of the company's cement plant, Rs. 16.57 crores have been drawn by way of bridging loans. An amount equivalent to Rs. 16.19 crores has been drawn against the foreign currency loans sanctioned by the International Finance Corporation Washington and the Indian Financial Institutions for financing expansion of the cement plant as well as for setting up the heavy engineering project at Hazira. Out of the amount of Rs. 27.50 crores raised in 1985 through the issue of 'B' series debentures, an amount of Rs. 25.00 crores has been utilised for working capital purposes."

This explains the manner finances have been raised by the company and how they have been deployed.

The directors' report also details matters of particular interest to shareholders such as dividends proposed, bonus and rights issues. They also discuss industrial relations details, resignations, and elections of directors and other similar matters that need to be mentioned and voted upon at annual general meetings.

A directors' report is therefore a valuable document and if read intelligently can give the reader a good grasp of the workings of the company, the problems faced, the direction it intends taking and its prospects.

2

THE AUDIT REPORT

The auditor represents the shareholders and it is his duty to report to the shareholders and the general public on the stewardship of the company by the directors and whether the financial statements presented do, in fact, present a true and fair view of the state of the company.

The audit report is thus a very important report as it is the only impartial report that a shareholder actually gets on the company. However, it is more often than not, not read. It is placed often in an obscure part of the annual report (especially so if it does certain many qualifications) and is glossed over more often than not in directors' reports such as was the case in Reliance Industries, 1986, report which reads "The notes to the accounts No. 13 and 14 referred to in the auditors report are self explanatory and therefore do not call for any further comment". A note such as this does not really cause a shareholder concern. It is likely he may not have thought much of it. However, if he had taken the trouble to delve further he would have examined the qualifications which were:

(a) The company had changed the method of accounting for disposal of waste generated in the course of production on cash basis. Had this not been done, the profits for the year would have been lower by Rs. 11.72 crores.

(b) The company had hitherto valued inventories at cost. The company had changed the method of valuation to cost or market value and had this not been done profits would have been higher by Rs. 5.10 crores.

The company declared a profit in 1987 of Rs. 14.17 crores. If the company had followed a consistent method of accounting the profit would have reduced by Rs. 6.62 crores to Rs. 7.55 crores—a reduction of 46%; not an inconsiderable amount. Another point also comes to mind. The company has changed its method of valuing stock from cost to the lower of cost or market as a consequence of which the company lost Rs. 5.10 crores. This means that Rs. 5 crores worth of the company's stock is valued at less than what it cost the company to purchase it in the first place. The questions arise—how much more is there? Why and how has this arisen? Are there obsolete stocks?

Corn Products Co. (India) Ltd.'s auditors' S.B. Billimoria & Co. state in its report for the year ended September 30, 1986, "The company has changed the basis of accounting of advertising and publicity materials, advertising film prints and market research expenditure ..... Such expenses which were hitherto treated as expenditure of the year in which they were incurred have been treated as forming part of the closing stock or deferred revenue expenditure. As a result of these changes, the profit for the year is higher by Rs. 8,43,786.

"The company has changed the method of computation of depreciation with retrospective effect. The excess provision in respect of earlier years has been treated as income for the year. As a result the profit for the year is higher by Rs. 39,64,959.

"In respect of sundry debtors on whom legal action has been taken by the company, we are, on the basis of the evidence made available to us pending the outcome of the action taken by the company, unable to form an opinion on the recoverability or otherwise of Rs. 7,54,909 included in sundry debtors and the consequential effect, if any, on the profit for the year and reserves."

Exhibit 'I'

Corn Products Ltd.

(Rs. in crores)

Profit for the year to September 30, 1986	56.79
Less: (i) effect of change of basis of accounting of advertising and publicity materials, advertising film prints and market research expenditure	8.44
(ii) effect of change in the method of computation of depreciation	40.15
(iii) effect of providing for doubtful debts	7.55
Restated profit for the year	0.65

It would be observed from perusing exhibit I that had the adjustments mentioned not been made the profit would have been not Rs. 56.79 lakhs but a modest Rs. 0.7 lakhs (this is including a provision in full for doubtful debts).

The auditors qualified the financial statements of Indian Rayon in 1986-87 stating—

(i) Non provision for gratuity liability of Rs. 436.69 lakhs.
(ii) The increased rupee liability of Rs. 648.95 lakhs consequent on the realignment of the rupee value in terms of foreign currency values has not been adjusted in the accounts".

The company made a profit in the year to June 30, 1987 of Rs. 1,229 lakhs. Had provision in full been made for the two mentioned, the profit would have reduced to a mere Rs. 144 lakhs.

The auditor's report of Star Textiles is worthy of mention. Its qualifications are numerous and include:

1. Non adjustment of interest on deferred transaction of the company—amount unascertained.
2. Non provision of the following:
   (a) Depletion in the value of investment Rs. 12,40,000.
   (b) Sundry debtors and advances considered doubtful Rs. 44,40,037.
   (c) Interest Rs. 26,27,212.
3. Depreciation in respect of extra shift allowance amounting to Rs. 17,26,636 (aggregate to date Rs. 97,71,356) relating to plant and machinery not being provided for.
4. Non payment of Rs. 70,03,358 in respect of provident fund, employees state insurance tax deducted at source and other government dues.

The company is in very bad times. Its loss in the year ended December 31, 1985 was Rs. 1.94 crores. This was without mentioning the points mentioned. Had they and the others detailed in the report been taken into account the results would have been very much worse.

The auditors of Gangappa Industries Ltd., Nataraja Iyer & Co. made the following comments in its accounts as on 30 June 1986.

(a) No provision has been made towards interest if any on loan and penal interest on over due interest and instalment by a company and the financial institution. Amount not determined

(b) No provision for excise duty has been made amounting to Rs. 5,59,516 as claimed by the department.

The company had made a loss of Rs. 69 lakhs in the year. Had these been provided for the loss would have been possibly over Rs. 1 crore (assuming the interest cost being around Rs. 25 lakhs at least).

Great Eastern Shipping Co. Ltd. published a profit before tax of Rs. 7.08 crores for the year to 30 June 1986. This fact was well heralded as the shipping industry has been going through troubled times and was a tremendous improvement in the previous years profit of Rs. 1.89 crores. The auditors of Great Eastern qualified the published accounts for the non provision of the following:

(a) anticipated income tax liability of Rs. 1 crore

(b) gratuity to the crew—the liability of which was indeterminate.

(c) trade bills of Rs. 1.45 crores co-accepted by United Industrial Bank which had been repudiated by the bank.

Gratuity is often in many companies, accounted for on a cash basis. If (a) & (c) above had been accounted for, the profit would have reduced by Rs. 2.45 crores to Rs. 5.63 crores—a reduction of 34%.

The auditors of Larsen & Toubro Ltd. are Sharp & Tannan. They stated in the Larsen & Toubro Ltd. annual report for 1985-86 that—

(a) No provision had been made in the accounts in respect of liability for future payment of gratuity to certain employees of the company-gross Rs. 1,30.10 lakhs.

Had provision been made the effect would have been as follows:

The profit would be lower by 13.67 lakhs (net after income tax saving of Rs. 6.83) lakhs and further

(i) Reserves would be lower by Rs. 65.05 lakhs (net after income tax savings)

(ii) Current liabilities and provisions would be higher by Rs. 65.05 lakhs.

The auditors of Terpene Industries Ltd. which made a loss of Rs. 39.13 lakhs in the year to June 30, 1986 made the statement "No provision has been made for gratuity liabilities of Rs. 79,181 based on actuarial valuation. This has resulted in the under statement of loss by Rs. 11,872 and over statement of general research by Rs. 29,181. The auditors of DCM Ltd. made a similar comment in the report for 1986. "In accordance with the accounting policy followed by the company, no provision has been made for gratuity as at June 30, 1986 estimated at Rs. 1,287.23 lakhs. If provision had been made, taking into account future tax benefit the profit after tax would have been lower by Rs. 163.41 lakhs and the reserves would have been lower by a similar amount."

The auditors of Orson Electronics Co. which had published a profit before tax for the year to August 31, 1986 of Rs. 2,75,11,964, Ratan S. Mama & Co. stated in its report.

(a) Depreciation has been provided on straight line method on a pro-rata basis on assets acquired during the year as against depreciation for the full year being provided in the past. As a result of the change the depreciation for the year is lower by Rs. 14.02 lakhs and the profit for the year is higher by the same.

(b) Research and development expenses, which were higher to written off have been capitalised towards Orson Chassis expenses and these expenses are being amortised over a period of seven years. Accordingly, an amount of Rs. 31.87 lakhs is being carried forward under fixed assets and as a result of such change in the accounting policy, the profit for the year is higher to that extent.

(c) Closing inventory has been valued at cost including interest attributable to such inventory whereby interest of Rs. 31.92 lakhs has been included in the closing inventory. Had closing inventory been valued without including interest as was done in the previous year. the profit for the year would have been lower by Rs. 31.92 lakhs.

(d) No provision has been made in the accounts for outstanding gratuity liability actuarially determined at Rs. 6.04 lakhs, including Rs. 2.80 lakhs for the year.

The company was by innovativeness and by changing its method of accounting able to increase in paper its profits by Rs. 80.61 lakhs which is about 41% above the profit that should have been of Rs. 194.51 lakhs (see exhibit II). This would not have compared favourably to the previous years profit of Rs. 328.93 lakhs.

Exhibit 'II'

Orson Electronics Company Ltd.

			(Rs. in lakhs)
Profit for the year ended August 31, 1986			275.12
Less: (i) effect of change of basis of accounting for			
(a) depreciation	14.02		
(b)	31.87	45.89	
(ii) effect of interest capitalised		31.92	
(iii) gratuity liability for year not provided		2.80	80.61
			194.51

The auditors of DCM Ltd. had apart from the note on gratuity also made the following remarks:

1. In accordance with the accounting policy followed by the company, no provision has been made for the bonus payable to employees for 1985-86 estimated at Rs. 299.50 lakhs. The bonus charged in the current year relating to the previous year amounts to Rs. 314.24 lakhs. If provision had been made, including taking into account the future tax benefit, the profit for the year would have been higher by Rs. 7.37 lakhs and the reserves would have been lower by Rs. 149.75 lakhs.
2. The price of levy sugar sold after February 22, 1974, amounting to Rs. 799.03 lakhs is the subject of court cases and will require adjustment.
3. No provision has been made for doubtful debts and

loans. Had provisions on loans and advances been made taking into account future tax benefit, the profit after tax would have been lower by Rs. 97.39 lakhs and the reserves would have been lower by Rs. 97.39 lakhs.

4. No provision has been made for the net assets situated in Pakistan of Rs. 250.17 lakhs.

Had adjustments been made, the profit would have altered considerably.

"Attention is invited to note no. 8 of Schedule 18," state the auditors of Surat Cotton Spinning and Weaving Mills (year to June 30, 1986) dealing with the provision for depreciation in the accounts —due to a change in the method of calculation of depreciation for the year under review and the non provision of multiple shift allowance of Rs. 78.22 lakhs in respect of the financial year 1984-85 which would have reduced the reserves had it been provided. The company had made a profit in that year of only Rs. 11.04 lakhs. Had this charge been made the company would have had to declare a loss of Rs. 63.17 lakhs. It is interesting to note the company declared a dividend of Rs. 24.60 lakhs. This, in effect means that the company had inspite of suffering a loss paid a dividend out of accumulated reserves and was thus, in fact, eroding its net worth.

It is stated by the auditors of Mahindra Ugine Steel Co. Ltd., in the company's annual report for the year to June 30, 1986 "Loans and advances considered good include Rs. 32,06,066 advanced to the provident fund and gratuity funds .... in respect of which we, on the basis of evidence made available to us are unable to express an opinion on the recoverability or otherwise and the consequential effect, if any, in the reserves. The company has an investment of Rs. 12,00,000 in equity shares of Orissa Sponge Iron Ltd. and has given a loan of Rs. 2,36,000 to it. In the opinion of the directors no loss would arise in respect of these items for which a provision is necessary. We are unable to express an opinion on the matter". The comments are clear and unambiguous. If proper provisions had been made the profit would have reduced by Rs. 47 lakhs—a considerable figure.

Auditors Batliboi & Purohit state, in the annual report of Pune Chemicals Ltd.

"The company has filed a writ petition before the High Court of Jammu & Kashmir challenging the decision of the department in respect of levy of Central sales tax. Nonetheless, the company has provided the entire liability in this respect. However, the company has not made any provision in respect of interest amounting to Rs. 55,672.

No provision has been made on resin aggregating to Rs. 66,79,930 and liability of Rs. 98,10,666."

Although the company may win the case, the reader is made aware of a possible liability and can thus base his decision (for whatever purpose) armed with this knowledge.

Provisions are not made or accounting principles are changed often to show a better picture of the company and to make the performance appear to be satisfactory or improved. It is the audit report that draws the attention of the reader to the subtleties of "creativity" and informs him of what the facts actually are. The reader would be foolhardy to ignore the audit report because it informs him of the truth.

THE FINANCIAL STATEMENTS

The Financial Statements of the Company in an Annual Report comprises of the Balance Sheet as at the end of the accounting year and the Profit and Loss Account which summarises the activities of the company for the period of the Annual Report.

Nivya Limited
Balance Sheet as at December 31, 1989

		(in Rupees)	
		1989	1988
I. Sources of Funds			
1. Shareholder's funds			
(a) Capital		500	500
(b) Reserves		450	400
		950	900
2. Loan funds			
(a) Secured Loans		750	675
(b) Unsecured loans		400	325
		1,150	1,000
	Total ...	2,100	1,900
II. Application of funds			
3. Fixed assets			
(a) Gross block		2,300	2,050
(b) *Less:* Depreciation		600	550
		1,700	1,500
(c) Capital work in progress		120	100
		1,820	1,600
4. Investments		200	200

		1989	1988
5.	Current assets, loans & advances		
	(a) Incentives	600	400
	(b) Trade debtors	750	500
	(c) Sundry debtors	15	10
	(d) Prepaid expenses	10	5
	(e) Cash and bank balances	10	15
	(f) Other current assets	15	10
	(g) Loans and advances	200	160
		1,600	1,100
Less:			
6.	Current liabilities & provisions		
	(a) Trade creditors	550	280
	(b) Accrued expenses	10	5
	(c) Sundry creditors	100	85
	(d) Provisions	860	630
		1,520	1,000
7.	Net—current assets (5-6)	80	100
	Total ...	2,100	1,900

The Balance Sheet

A Company is a body distinct from the shareholders who own it. It is a separate legal entity. It can sue in its name, own property and do all other acts that a person can do.

The Balance Sheet reveals the financial position of a company on a particular date; of a company's assets (that which the company owns) and liabilities (that which the company owes) appropriately grouped under various categories.

It must be remembered that as a Balance Sheet comprises of the balances on a particular day these balances can and are capable of being materially different the next day as a consequence of which the perusal of the Balance Sheet may result in the reader arriving at totally different conclusions than which he would have arrived at the previous day. This can be illustrated by an example. Puniya Ltd. had a loan on September 30, 1989 of Rs. 10,000. On the Balance Sheet at September 30, 1989 this loan was shown. As the loan was repayable on October 1, 1989 there was adequate cash to repay the loan.

On September 30, 1989, the Balance Sheet of Puniya Ltd. was as follows.

Puniya Ltd.
Balance Sheet as at September 30, 1989

			(in Rupees)
Shareholders funds	5,000	Fixed Assets	6,000
Loan Funds	10,000	Investments	1,000
Current Liabilities	3,000	Current Assets	11,000
	18,000		18,000

On October 1, 1989, the loan was repaid. The Balance Sheet at the close of business on that day read:

Puniya Ltd.
Balance Sheet as at October 1, 1989

			(in Rupees)
Shareholders funds	5,000	Fixed Assets	6,000
Loan Funds	—	Investments	1,000
Current Liabilities	3,000	Current Assets	1,000
	8,000		8,000

An analyst or reader reviewing the two Balance Sheets would, on analysis, arrive at diametrically different conclusions. On September 30, 1989, it would appear that Puniya Ltd. is a highly leveraged company—a company highly dependant on borrowed funds as a source of capital. It would also be termed as extremely cash rich or liquid as it has more than enough current assets to pay its current liabilities and them some.

The Balance Sheet as at October 1, 1989 portrays a totally different picture. The company would appear to be conservatively financed—the management preferring to source its finance from internal generation and shareholders than from external borrowings. The company would also be viewed as illiquid as the company's current liabilities far exceed its current assets.

A feature of the Balance Sheet is that it must balance. The total liabilities including the shareholder's funds must equal the total assets. This is based on the logic that if an asset is utilised either another asset must increase or a liability should decrease. This is the basis of the concept of double entry and is illustrated in the following examples.

Example A: Puniya Ltd. purchased a machine for Rs. 1,00,000/-. In order to purchase the machine, the company borrowed Rs. 90,000/- from a bank and the balance was paid from its current account at a bank.

As a consequence of this transaction Puniya's

  (i) Fixed Assets will increase by   Rs. 1,00,000
 (ii) Liabilities (Loans) will increase by   Rs.   90,000
(iii) Current Assets (Cash at Bank) will
     decrease by   Rs.   10,000

Example B: Puniya Ltd. purchased raw materials worth Rs. 50,000 for its factory on credit.

This transaction would result in Puniya's

 (i) Current Assets (Stock) increasing by   Rs. 50,000
(ii) Current Liabilities (Trade Creditors)
    increasing by   Rs. 50,000

Sources of funds:

A company, any company must have finance to fund its activities—to purchase machinery for the manufacture of its products, to purchase land for its factory, to lease offices to house its personnel and to purchase raw materials. The amount of finance that a company would require would depend on its size, its nature, its location, and the manner in which it proposes to grow.

How does a company raise its funds? What are its sources? A company can raise funds from its shareholders or by borrowing:

1. SHAREHOLDERS' FUNDS

A company sources funds from its shareholders by either the issue of shares (share capital) or by the plough back of profits (reserves). In short, shareholders' funds represent the stake the shareholders have in the company—the investment they have made.

Share Capital

Share capital represents the shares issued to the public by the company. However, prior to the issuance of share capital the Memorandum of Association of the company must "authorise" the shares. The amount authorised would depend entirely on the promoters' estimate of the funds required by the business to purchase its assets and fund its working capital.

Share capital is issued in a number of ways:

(i) *Private Placement:* This is by offering the shares of the company not to the public at large but to selected individuals or institutions.

(ii) *Public issue:* Shares are offered to the public at large through a prospectus. This is the most common, most popular and probably the most effective way of raising share capital. Often, especially for a popular issue, (such as the Reliance or the Garden Vareli or the BPL or the Videocon issue) the issue is many times oversubscribed. In these situations all the applicants may not receive shares. The shares are allotted based on a formula arrived at in conjunction (for impartiality) with the stock exchange of the city where the company is based or where the share will be primarily quoted.

(iii) *Rights issue:* The shareholders are offered as a "matter of right" shares in the company in proportion to the holding that they have in i.e. one right share for every four shares held. These are extremely popular as the rights shares are usually offered to the shareholders at a price much lower than the market value of the shares. In November 1987, Reliance Industries Limited offered its shareholders rights shares at Rs. 60 each whereas at that time, its shares were being quoted in the market at around Rs. 120 per share. The shareholder stands to make an immediate profit on shares issued in this manner.

(iv) *Bonus issue:* In a bonus issue, no monies are raised. Existing reserves such as the premium on shares issued or profit ploughed back are capitalised or converted to

24

bonus shares. These too, are issued to shareholders in proportion to the shares they already own. Unlike rights issues, a shareholder cannot refuse a bonus issue. It must be remembered that after a *bonus issue*, the pattern of shareholding will not change as bonus shares are issued in proportion to existing shareholding. The main purpose of bonus issues are apart from pleasing the shareholders by giving them additional shares, to widen and strengthen the capital base so that the foundation for growth is tangible, real and solid.

A company issues, nowadays two kinds of shares:

(i) *Preference shares:* This is really a misnomer as most persons do not "prefer" these shares. It is more to the contrary. They avoid them and presently it is very rare for companies to issue these shares.

Preference shares carry the right of a fixed rate of dividend every year and if the company does not make a profit, this dividend accumulates. Normally dividends to preference shareholders must be paid prior to that paid to other shareholders. Preference shareholders have also a 'preferential' claim on the assets of the company in the event of a winding up or liquidation. Being safer than ordinary or equity shares and to counter balance its advantages, the preference shareholder does not have the right to vote at Annual General Meetings or to decide company policy.

(ii) *Ordinary or equity shares:* The ordinary or equity shareholders are the real owners of a company. They bear the risks and enjoy the benefits. In a bad year when the company has made little or no profits, they receive no dividends. Conversely, in a good times they receive large dividends and bonus shares. These shareholders are the ones entitled to vote and decide on company policy. At a time of liquidation, they divide among themselves the assets left over after all others including the preference shareholders have been paid. They stand to lose their investment if there are no assets left after the others have been paid off. On the other hand, they stand too, to make a lot of money if the assets remaining are far in excess of their original investments as the balance would be divided equally between the ordinary shareholders.

Reserves

Reserves are profits or gains retained in the business for growth and expansion.

Reserves are divided into two—capital reserves and revenue reserves.

Capital Reserves: Capital reserves are reserves that have resulted from the increase in the value of assets. These are not freely distributable to members as dividends and may be used only for certain specific reasons. The most common capital reserve is the share premium account. This arises from the sale of shares at a "premium" (a price higher than its face value). In November 1987, Reliance Industries Ltd. had a right issue where at it issued to its members Rs. 10 shares at a price of Rs. 60 per share. The premium per share of Rs. 50 was credited to a share premium account. This reserve may be used only for certain specific purposes such as the writing off of preliminary or share issue expenses, issuing bonus shares or providing for the premium payable on the redemption of preference shares and debentures. Another capital reserve that is usually found in Balance Sheets is the Capital Revaluation Reserve. This arises when assets acquired many years earlier such as land is revalued at current market prices. The unrealised gain on revaluation creates the revaluation reserve. This can only be extinguished when the gain is realised i.e. the property revalued is sold. In 1940 Puniya Ltd. purchased land for a factory in Andheri Bombay for Rs. 50,000. In 1989 it revalued the land which was worth by then Rs. 10,000,000/-. In order to reflect current values it was decided that the land should be shown on the Balance Sheet at current values. The difference of Rs. 9,950,000 was thus shown as a capital reserve.

2. LOAN FUNDS

Apart from raising funds for expansion and growth from its

shareholders, the only other way of raising capital is by borrowing money from the public.

Borrowing monies is usually preferred to raising capital from shareholders as it is relatively easier and the rules that have to be complied with are comparatively minimal.

If a company wishes to raise capital by issuing shares it must approach its existing shareholders as they have the right to be offered the new shares and to accept them so as to continue to maintain their proportionate ownership of the company. Even prior to such an offer being made the approval of the controller of capital issues must be obtained and the resolution to issue shares must be approved by the members in an extraordinary meeting. It is expensive to issue shares too as there are many share issue expenses such as advertisements; the printing of prospectuses and the likes. Then the cost of servicing the new capital may be higher than the interest to be paid on debentures.

It is therefore much easier for a company to borrow funds and it may borrow as much as is authorised by its Memorandum of Association.

Loans may be divided into Secured loans and Unsecured loans.

1. Secured Loans

Secured loans are those loans that have been taken by a company by pledging some of its assets such as land, buildings, stocks and debtors. The usual secured loans that a company has are debentures, bank overdrafts and long term loans taken from banks or financial institutions for the purchase of machinery or some other long term asset.

2. Unsecured Loans

Unsecured loans are loans taken by the company for which the company has not pledged any of its assets. The security a lender has is usually the credit worthiness of the company. These are usually fixed deposits and short term loans. At times banks give overdrafts against which they are not required to hypothecate stocks or debtors. These are known as clear overdrafts and shown as unsecured loans.

Another distinction that is made on loan funds is whether they are current or funded. Current loans are those that are payable in one year whereas funded are those that are payable only at the expiry of one year. Current loans will include too all demand loans i.e. loans repayable at demand such as overdrafts.

3. FIXED ASSETS

Fixed assets are those assets that a company owns for use in its business. They are not purchased for resale but for producing the products made by the company (factory and machinery), warehousing the products (godowns and warehouses), transporting them (trucks, tempos etc.), to house the offices (office buildings) and the likes.

Every company will have some fixed assets. This truth was mentioned by Adam Smith when he stated in the *Wealth of Nations*, "Some part of capital of every master artifier or manufacturer must be fixed in the instrument of his trade".

The kind of fixed assets a company would own would vary enormously from company to company and from trade to trade. A manufacturing company's major fixed assets would be its factory and machinery whereas that of service industry would be its office building. Similarly a transportation company's major fixed assets would be its trucks.

Fixed assets are normally shown on the Balance Sheet at cost. If a machine was purchased in 1984 for Rs. 2,000,000, it would be shown at this price in 1989 too if it is still used in the business. This has created some controversy in some learned accounting circles where it is argued that these assets should be shown, on the Balance Sheet, at current replacement value or current cost value as opposed to historical cost. This, it is argued, would be more appropriate as all other assets and liabilities are shown at current values.

Often land and other assets are revalued. This is done to show actual values of assets and this is useful in situations where original cost and current values are widely different. In 1945, Puniya Limited purchased an acre of land near Powai, Bombay for Rs. 2000. This was the value shown in the book of the company till 1989 when it was revalued. At that time the price was not Rs. 2000 but Rs. 15,000,000. The Company had, in short, really been having a hidden reserve of Rs. 14,998,000. The asset was then written up to its realisable value. However, the increase in value of Rs. 14,998,000 cannot be distributed to the members until the land is sold. Therefore the increase in value is transferred to a capital reserve called revaluation reserve till such time as the sale of this property takes place.

Depreciation

"The only certainty in life is that if you are born you are bound to die." This is true. All persons have a life span. Machines and fixed assets being manmade are similarly mortal. After a period of use they wear down and become of no use.

Depreciation accounts for the wear and tear of machinery and other assets and attempts to reduce the value of the asset equally over its useful life and at the same time sets aside from profits the amount of the estimated wearing down so that by the time the asset has been utilised for its full life or tenure, there would have been set aside from profits an amount equal to the original cost of the asset and this could be utilised to purchase another. However, in these days of inflation and rising prices this is not usually possible as costs have quadrupled. Some companies to counter this, create an additional depreciation reserve which would amount to the difference between the original cost and present cost of a similar asset. There is no hard or fast rule of depreciation and companies are normally free to choose the kind of depreciation they would like to adopt. The more common methods are:

(i) Straight line method

Under this method depreciation is provided in equal amounts every year in a manner by which at the end of the useful life of the article, the total accumulated depreciation would be equal to the original cost of the asset.

In 1983 Puniya Ltd. purchased a motor vehicle which it intended to write off over a period of 5 years for Rs. 100,000. Under the straight line method depreciation would be

Rs. 20,000 every year and at the end of 5 years the accumulated depreciation would equal cost.

(ii) Reducing Balance Method

Under the reducing balancing method depreciation is not calculated on the cost but on written down value. If Puniya Ltd. had purchased a vehicle for Rs. 100,000 and it is to be written off over 5 years, in the 1st year depreciation would be Rs. 20,000. In the second year, depreciation would be 20% of Rs. 80,000. In the third year it would be less. Under this method an asset will never be fully written off as depreciation is always calculated on a reducing balance.

Many industries work for more than one shift in a day. As the useful life in calendar months will be less for a machine that works two shifts as opposed to another that only works one, those that work two or more shifts normally provide double shift depreciation.

There are a few other methods of depreciation such as the interest method and the rule of 72 but these are not commonly used.

Land is the only fixed asset that is never depreciated as it usually appreciates in value. The costs of leased premises are written off over the period of the lease. Buildings are normally depreciated over forty years.

Capital work in progress

On the Balance Sheet date, there are normally many projects that are not complete and functioning. These may relate to the construction of a factory or the installation of machineries. As the work is in progress and is of a capital nature, this is known as "capital work in progress."

Capital work in progress is shown at cost. It is not depreciated as it is not a fully functional asset. Once complete it would be broken down to type such as machinery, equipment etc. and depreciated.

INVESTMENTS

Investments are the purchases of shares or debentures or units purchased by a company for earning income and to utilise profitably surplus cash funds. These investments are not usually related in any manner to the business of the company, nor are they purchased for trading nor is the company dependant on these for the daily conduct of its affairs. These usually represent the deployment of short term surplus funds.

Investments may be divided into three—

(a) Trade

Trade investments are shares or debentures held of competitors or others in similar businesses. Many companies have nominal holdings in their competitor companies. This is done to have access to information on their growth, profitability and other pertinent matters.

(b) Subsidiary and Associate Companies

Companies hold shares in their subsidiary and associate companies. The United Breweries Group and the Tata Group are prime examples of groups that have an intricate crossownership of group companies.

(c) Others

There are shares or debentures or other security held that is not in any way trade or subsidiary investments. It is in this category that companies invest their surplus cash for profit and income.

Investments are usually detailed in the schedules to the Annual Report where at all their particulars are stated. They are normally divided into quoted and unquoted investments.

(i) *Quoted Investments:* are those shares/debentures that are quoted in a recognised stock exchange and are freely traded.

(ii) *Unquoted Investments:* are shares of companies (usually private) that are not quoted in a recognised stock exchange.

Investments are valued at the lower of cost or market value. The valuation of quoted shares are relatively easy as the closing prices are published in the newspapers and magazines. Such a valuation is not available for unquoted investments. They are valued in differing ways—the most common being the net assets of the company being divided by the number of shares issued in order to arrive at the value per share. The value of a share can also be arrived at by dividing the net realisable value of all assets by the number of shares issued.

CURRENT ASSETS, LOANS AND ADVANCES

Current assets are those assets that a company owns that are used in the normal business of the company or are generated by the company such as debtors and finished stock into cash or cash equivalent within a reasonable time. In practice any assets that are turned into cash within a year is considered a current asset.

It is important to remember that the business of a company would decide whether an asset is current or fixed. A computer would be a current asset to a computer dealer or manufacturer while it would be a fixed asset to most others. The reasons are self-explanatory. Similarly an Ambassador motor car would be a current asset to companies such as Hindustan Motors or a car dealer whereas to most commercial concerns it would be a fixed asset.

Current assets may be divided into two:

(i) *Converting:* Converting assets are those that are produced in the normal course of business such as finished goods and debtors (when sold)

(ii) *Cash equivalent:* These are those assets that are in the form of cash or cash equivalents. They can be utilised to repay dues. The common cash equivalent assets are cash in hand and at the bank and short term investments.

(a) Stocks (Inventories):

Stocks are the most important current assets held by a company. They consist usually of —

(a) *Raw materials:* The primary purchase which is utilised to manufacture the product/products the company makes.

(b) *Work in progress:* Similar to capital work in progress

32

this represents goods that are in the process of manufacture but are yet to be complete.

(c) *Finished goods:* The product/products manufactured by the company that are ready for sale but are yet to be sold.

(d) *Loose tools and spare parts:* These are important to production and represent tools and spares for machines. Their consumption is consequently slow.

Stocks are subject to enormous manipulation and have been the subject of many practitioners of creative accountants. It is important therefore to consider the method of how the value has been arrived at. Stocks are valued at the lower of cost or market value or realisable value. This is to ensure that there will be no loss at the time of sale as that would have been accounted for.

(i) *FIFO or First in first out:* Under this method of valuation it is assumed that the stocks that come in first will be sold first and so on. If Puniya Limited purchased 30 bags of cement for Rs. 1500/- on January 1, 1989 and another 20 bags of cement in March 1989 for Rs. 1200/- and has on June 30, 1989 40 bags left the value of the stocks would be:

(a) 20 bags at Rs.50/- each	Rs. 1000
(b) 20 bags at Rs. 60/- each	Rs. 1200
	Rs. 2200

(ii) *LIFO or Last in first out:* This method is based on a premise totally the opposite of FIFO. Under this scheme it would be assumed that the stocks that arrive last will be sold first. The argument is that customers prefer new materials or products. If we utilise, the example given above, the value of Puniya Ltd.'s stocks on June 30, 1989 would be:

(a) 30 bags at Rs.50/- each	Rs. 1500
(b) 10 bags at Rs. 60/- each	Rs. 600
	Rs. 2100

At this moment the difference may not appear high. However, at a time of rising prices, the figure on the Balance Sheet would not be truly reflective of its actual value. This is why FIFO is the more popular method.

(b) Trade Debtors:

Most companies do not sell their products for cash. In a competitive environment most customers expect credit i.e. some time to pay for the items purchased. Trade debtors therefore represent the amount due from customers on the Balance Sheet date.

The amount of credit extended would vary from company to company and customer to customer. The usual period of credit given is for 30 days. It is not unusual however to extend credit for 60 days or 90 days. Often, even in spite of this customers delay in paying their dues. In order therefore to provide the reader an insight of the effectiveness of the administration of credit and to give early warnings of possible bad debts companies are required to divide debtors as—

(a) Over six months and

(b) Others.

As stated earlier, all customers may not pay for their goods. Some may have gone bankrupt; others may have amounts in dispute; others may simply just not want to pay. It is important that readers be aware of the realisability of debts and to enable them to be aware, debts are clasified as—

(i) Debts considered good

(ii) Debts considered bad and doubtful.

Prudence dictates that the company should provide for debts that are likely to be bad. This provision is necessary as if it is not debtors as an asset would be overstated i.e. shown on the Balance Sheet at a figure higher than its realisable value.

The provision is calculated in the following ways (It may be a combination of both too):

(i) Specific—the debts likely to be bad and doubtful are listed and examined and a provision is made for the

34

amounts that are unlikely to be realised. Numba Ltd. owed Puniya Ltd. Rs. 10,000. Of this, it was believed that Numba would only pay back Rs. 6000. In this situation a specific provision for Rs. 4000 should be made.

(ii) General—a general provision is created on the basis of past experience. In earlier years about 3% of all debtors may not have paid for one reason or another. On the strength of this trend, a general provision of 3% on all amounts due may be made. This would act as a cushion on debts that turn sour.

(c) Prepaid expenses:

All payments are not made when due. Many payments (especially in the service industry) are made in advance. These may be quarterly, half yearly or annually such as rent payments, premiums on insurance policies and the likes. The amount paid in advance and which pertains to a period after the Balance Sheet date is shown as pre-paid expenses. On July, 1, 1989 Puniya Ltd. paid Rs. 100,000 as annual contract fees for the maintenance of certain machines. At December 31, 1989, Puniya Ltd. would have, on its Balance Sheet, prepaid expenses of Rs. 50,000 which is that part of the maintenance fee per-taining to the six months to June 30, 1990.

(d) Cash and Bank Balance:

Cash in hand and in petty cash boxes, tills and the likes and the balances on a company's current accounts are shown under this heading in a company's Balance Sheet.

These are the most liquid of a company's asset and it is important that these be regularly checked and moni-tored.

(e) Other Current Assets:

Other current assets are all amounts due that are re-coverable within the next twelve months. These are usually interest due on investments made, claims receiv-able and the likes.

LOANS AND ADVANCES

Loans are amounts lent which are repayable within a certain

period of time. These may be to other companies or to individuals like staff members to whom loans for housing and personal purposes are frequently given.

Advances are amounts paid in advance. These may be to raw material suppliers to supply raw materials or to others such as contractors etc. Puniya Ltd. had given an advance of Rs. 800,000 for the supply of steel to a supplier. As the steel had not been supplied upto the Balance Sheet date, the advance of Rs. 800,000 would be shown as an advance.

CURRENT LIABILITIES & PROVISIONS:

Current liabilities are amount due and payable by the company within the next twelve months. Provisions on the other hand are amounts set aside for a likely payment or expense which is estimated and likely to be incurred.

Trade Creditors:

Trade Creditors are those from whom a company purchases its raw materials and other articles that are used in the production of its products. There is usually an amount due as most suppliers extend a period of credit. The terms and tenure of credit would differ from company to company. Trade creditors are shown on the Balance Sheet at the amount due to them less any advance paid (Puniya Ltd. had paid an advance of Rs.2,00,000 to a supplier on November 15, 1989. On December 31, 1989, the Supplier had effected delivery of items valued at Rs. 750,000. On December 31, trade creditors would amount to Rs. 550,000.

Accrued Expenses

Many expenses are paid for after they are incurred such as electricity, telephone, salaries, interest on bank overdrafts and the likes. This is because it is difficult to bill for certain expenses in advance. These are also difficult to estimate as there can be wide fluctuations. The expenses incurred that are unpaid at the date of the Balance Sheet are shown as accrued expenses.

Puniya Ltd.'s telephone bill is usually about Rs. 2500 every two months. Puniya had paid its telephone bills upto November 30, 1989. In this situation an estimated accrual of Rs. 1250 (1 month's expense) would be accrued on

December 31, 1989 under the head "accrued expenses"..

Sundry Creditors:

Any other amounts due are usually clubbed under the all-embracing title of sundry creditors. These are usually interest accrued on interest, unclaimed dividends and the likes.

Provisions:

Provisions are amounts set aside from profits to meet a likely payment or expense. The normal provisions that one would normally see on the Balance Sheet are "proposed dividend" and "Taxation".

Nivya Limited
Profit & Loss Account for the year ended 31 December 1989

		1989	1988
			(in Rupees)
INCOME			
7.	Sales	9,000	7,000
8.	Other income	300	250
		9,300	7,250
EXPENDITURE			
9.	Materials	4,600	3,800
10.	Employment	1,950	1,725
11.	Operating and other expenses	1,050	575
12.	Interest and finance charges	175	150
13.	Depreciation	50	40
		7,825	6,290
	Profit for the year before tax	1,475	960
14.	Taxation	600	450
	Profit after tax:	875	510
APPROPRIATIONS			
15.	Proposed dividend	100	100
16.	General reserves	200	100
		300	200
	Balance carried forward	575	310

PROFIT AND LOSS ACCOUNT:

The Profit and Loss Account summarises the working of a company over a period of time which may be a month, six months, a year or longer. It informs the reader of the income earned, the expenditure incurred and states the result whether it be a profit or a loss at the end of the period. It is in effect the translation in rupees and paise of the effectiveness of the management's policies. It illustrates in figures the competence and foresight of the management, the quality and ability of the staff and the popularity of the product of the company. It shows whether the decision makers of the company actually know the market they are in; whether they can compete and hold their own and grow. It is in short the company's performance appraisal that is laid bare by the management of the company to its peers to judge their efforts.

1. SALES

Sales measures the inflow of assets from selling goods and providing services to third parties. Sales are accounted for after the ownership in goods and the consequent risks relating to these goods are passed to the customer in return for some consideration (usually cash). In normal circumstances the physical possession of the goods would also be transferred in that the goods would leave the company's warehouse and will be delivered to the customer. Sometimes, goods are placed by a company at the shop of a dealer with the understanding that payment need be made only after the goods are sold or they may be returned. In these circumstances, no sale has actually taken place and ownership and risk have not been transferred nor has any consideration been paid.

Companies do give trade discounts and other incentive discounts to customers to entice them to buy their product. Sales should be accounted for after these discounts.

Often goods sold to customers are returned—the reasons may be diverse. The value of goods returned must be reduced from sales.

There are many companies that deduct excise duty from sales. There are more companies who show this as an expense. In strict accounting it is preferable to show excise

38

duty as a deduction from sales as then the sales figures would reflect the actual markup made by the company on its cost of production.

2. OTHER INCOME:

Companies do receive income from sources other than the sale of their products. The normal items that appear under this title are—

(a) Profit from the sale of assets—this arises when the proceeds received on the sale of a fixed asset exceeds its written down value (cost less accumulated depreciation).

(b) Dividends—dividends earned from investments made by the company in the shares of other companies.

(c) Rent—rent received from commercial buildings and apartments leased from the company.

(d) Interest—interest received on deposits made and loans given to corporate bodies and others.

3. MATERIALS:

Materials are the raw materials and other components used in the manufacture of the company's products. These would include, in most cases, consumable stores and other materials used in production.

The cost of materials consumed or conversely the material cost of the products sold is arrived at by adding the purchases made in the year to the opening stock and deducting that from the closing stock.

4. EMPLOYMENT COSTS:

All the costs of employing staff are accounted for under employment costs. This includes apart from salaries and wages bonus, gratuity, contribution to provident and other funds, welfare expenses and other staff related expenditure.

5. OPERATING AND OTHER EXPENSES:

All the other costs incurred in running a company are operating and other expenses. These include—

(a) Selling expenses— the cost of advertising, sales promotion, commission paid to salesmen, cash discounts and all other expenses incurred to sell the company's products;

(b) Administration expenses— rent of offices and factories, municipal taxes, insurance, repairs, printing and stationery; telephone and telex costs, legal expenses, electricity costs and all other expenses to administer a company.

(c) Others—these are those costs that are not specific to either selling or administration such as the loss made on the sale of fixed assets and donations made by the company.

6. INTEREST AND FINANCE CHARGES:

When monies are borrowed from third parties (corporations, banks, financial institutions and individuals), interest has to be paid. The normal borrowings that a company pays interest on are—

(a) Bank overdrafts—monies extended by banks for working capital;

(b) Term Loans—borrowings from bank and financial institutions to purchase machinery;

(c) Fixed Deposits—fixed deposits taken from shareholders and the general public for working capital.

(d) Debentures—these are issued to shareholders and the general public for long term capital needs usually;

(e) Intercorporate Loans—often loans are taken from other companies for working capital purposes or to tide over a temporary cash deficiency.

Interest and finance charges are shown separately on the Profit and Loss Account as this would vary as a percentage from one company to another as the shareholders funds to borrowed funds of different companies would vary.

7. DEPRECIATION:

Depreciation is, as has been explained, the amount by which the fixed assets have suffered wear and tear during the year. This is also the amount set aside from profits so that when the existing asset has been written down entirely, there would be a provision equal to the cost of the asset which could be utilised to purchase another. As, on account of inflation, a machine cannot be bought at the price ruling four years earlier, many companies provide for an additional amount. This additional amount would however not be charged as depreciation (expense) but would be shown as an appropriation of profits (transfer to general reserves).

TAXATION

The third certainty in existence after life and death is taxation.

The major objective of a company is to maximise its profits and to grow at a rapid pace. However in this pursuit, whenever the company makes a profit, it has to pay tax on the income earned.

The taxable profit is different from the accounting profit. This is because many amounts legitimately expensed may not be tax deductible. Similarly under tax law certain allowances such as investment allowance etc. are received. This again is not to be included in the tax computations.

PROPOSED DIVIDENDS:

The dividends, given to shareholders is the reward given to them for investing in the company. In boom years the rewards may be great whereas in year of depression or recession they may not receive any dividends at all. This is why dividends are also known as the reward for risks taken by the investors or shareholders. As a normal rule smaller riskier companies pay high dividends whereas well established blue chip companies pay lower dividends.

Most companies pay dividends twice a year.

These are:—

(i) Interim dividends—these are paid during the year in anticipation of satisfactory results:

(ii) Final dividend—final dividends are normally declared after the results of the year have been arrived at. This is recommended by the Directors, discussed at the annual general meeting and paid after it has been approved by the members at the meeting.

41

GENERAL RESERVES:

Profits are appropriated and transferred to general reserves for various reasons such as ploughback, increasing shareholders funds and thus commitment, meet unexpected expenditure and provide funds to purchase machinery and other assets at a future date. These are revenue reserves and can be distributed to shareholders as dividends.

CONTINGENT LIABILITY:

A contingent liability is a liability that may arise on the happening of an event—the event itself may not happen. Company law and good accounting practice dictates that readers must also be aware of possible future liabilities that are contingent on the happening of an uncertain event so that they could consider the effect of this when attempting to arrive at an opinion on the financial condition of a company.

The contingent liabilities of a company are stated in the notes to the accounts and the normal ones that are stated in the case of most companies are:

(a) Bills discounted with banks— these may become liabilities should the bill be dishonoured.
(b) Gratuity to employees not provided for.
(c) Legal suits against the company not provided for.
(d) Excise claims against the company.

A person reading the accounts of a company would be wise to read the notes on contingent liabilities and make those adjustments that he feels may be relevant to the financial statements.

The Evolution of Financial Statements
A Guided Tour

Krishnan and Vinay were friends at the Engineering College in Bombay. On qualifying they went their separate ways— Krishnan to the Gulf and Vinay joined a multinational engineering company. Many years passed. Krishnan, by sheer chance, met Vinay at a restaurant. They talked of old times, the present and their future. They were at the stage of waiting to do something on their own. They talked and then talked some more and slowly began to think of starting an engineering company of their own manufacturing high precision instruments.

On January 1, 1989, they formed a company they named Vinkris Ltd. The company had an authorised share capital of 1,00,000 shares of Rs. 10 each. Krishnan and Vinay purchased for cash at par 30,000 shares.

The Balance Sheet on January 1, 1989 was as follows:

Share Capital		Current Assets	
Authorised	Rs. 10,00,000	Cash	Rs. 6,00,000
Issued	Rs. 6,00,000		
	Rs. 6,00,000		Rs. 6,00,000

The two investors approached their bankers for a loan for five years to purchase machinery and for overdraft facilities for working capital. The bankers authorised a term loan on January 28, 1989 of Rs. 10,00,000 and an overdraft limit of Rs. 15,00,000. Both these loans were secured—the former by the specific hypothecation of the machinery purchased and the latter by the hypothecation of stocks and debtors.

On February 1, 1989, the company took premises on rent at a monthly rent of Rs. 20,000. The rent was paid in advance for six months. A precision instruments making machine was purchased for Rs. 12,00,000 and installed on February 15, 1989. The company also purchased raw materials of Rs. 9,00,000 for cash.

Balance Sheet on February 28, 1989

Share holders' funds		Fixed assets	
Share capital	Rs. 6,00,000	Machinery	Rs. 12,00,000
Loan funds			
secured	Rs. 16,20,000	Current Assets	
		Stock	Rs. 9,00,000
		Cash	Nil
		Preliminary expenses (Rent)	Rs. 20,000
		Prepaid expenditure	Rs. 1,00,000
	Rs. 22,20,000		Rs. 22,20,000

43

On March 1, 1989 the company began making precision instruments. The company hired 50 workers at Rs. 300 per month and 10 office staff at an average salary of Rs. 1500 per month.

In the first three months the company sold Rs. 8,00,000 worth of precision instruments—the sale price being 40% over the cost of production (materials & labour cost). Of these only Rs. 4,50,000 have paid as yet. The company also purchased additional stock of Rs. 7,00,000 of which Rs. 4,00,000 has been paid for, the balance being payable by the end of June 1989.

The company also paid during the three months Rs. 50,000 for stationery, postage and travelling, Rs. 20,000 for transportation and Rs. 10,000 for repairs. Other miscellaneous costs totalled Rs. 10,000. All these were paid for in cash except for stationery of which Rs. 10,000 is still outstanding.

The financial statement at May 31, 1989 was as follows:—

Profit and Loss Account for the period to 31st May, 1989

	Rs.		Rs.
Materials	6,10,000	Sales	8,00,000
Labour	30,000		
Gross Profit carried			
down	1,60,000		
	Rs. 8,00,000		Rs. 8,00,000
Salaries	15,000	Gross Profit	
		brought down	1,60,000
Rent	60,000		
Postage, Stationery			
& Travelling	50,000		
Repairs	10,000		
Transportation	10,000		
Other Miscellaneous			
costs	10,000		
Depreciation	2,000		
Net Profit	3,000		
	Rs. 1,60,000		Rs. 1,60,000

Balance Sheet as at May 31, 1989

Shareholders funds	Rs.	Fixed Assets	Rs.
Share Capital	6,00,000	Cost	12,00,000
Reserves	3,000	Less depreciation	2,000
	6,03,000		11,98,000
Borrowed funds		**Current Assets**	
Term loan	10,00,000	Debtors	3,50,000
Bank Overdraft	6,85,000	Preliminary	
		expenses	20,000
		Stocks	9,90,000
		Prepaid expenses	40,000
	16,85,000		14,00,000
Current Liabilities			
Creditors	3,10,000		
TOTAL ...	25,98,000	TOTAL ...	25,98,000

The above have been illustrated to inform the reader on how financial statements evolve and how transactions are reflected on financial statements.

SCHEDULES AND NOTES TO THE ACCOUNTS

The Schedules and Notes to the Accounts are an integral part of the financial statements of a company. They detail the makeup of the assets and liabilities of the entity and it is of paramount importance that these be perused in detail at the time of reading financial statements. Most persons are normally averse to figures and abhor serious reading. They avoid scrutinising the schedules and reading the notes to the accounts. This is dangerous as by doing so pertinent and important details—details that could make or break the company might escape unread.

Share Capital

The Schedules normally commence with the analysis of shareholders' funds. The schedule details the authorised capital and the amount issued and paid up. This would allow the reader to be aware of how many more shares can be issued by the company. Many companies give additional information too such as—

(a) ITC Limited's statements included the information "of the above, following were allotted as fully paid up Bonus Shares:

3,790,000 in 1978-79 by capitalisation of capital reserve, share premium reserve and general reserve; 4,548,000 in 1980-81 by capitalisation of capital reserve and general reserve."

(b) Larsen & Toubro's 1985-86 statement has a disclosure:

	Rs. Lakhs
Equity shares of Rs. 10 each	51,99,33
Less: Calls in arrears	2,70
	51,96,63

The former gives an indication on when bonus shares were issued and probably makes one wonder whether the company may issue a bonus in the near future.

Larsen's statements inform the reader that there are arrears due on shares. The company can forfeit the shares not fully paid for.

Reserves

The Reserves are another important item that must be looked at. Reserves are broken down into capital Reserves (the share premium account, the capital revaluation reserve and the capital redemption reserve) and Revenue reserves (profit & loss account, general reserve and the likes).

The first concern of an investor would be to ascertain whether the company has adequate reserves to issue bonus shares. Bonus shares may be issued by capitalising any of the reserves except any capital reserve so long as the reserve has not come about by the revaluation of assets or without any receipt of cash. There are many other guidelines, the main ones being—

(a) The residual reserves after capitalisation should be

46

atleast 40% of the increased paid up capital;

(b) All contingent liabilities disclosed in the audited accounts which have a bearing on the net profits will have to be deducted in calculating the minimum residual reserves.

(c) The overall limit is that at any one time the amount capitalised should not exceed the total paid up equity capital of the company i.e. the maximum bonus issue can only be in the ratio of 1:1.

(d) A company may make an application only 12 months after the date of sanction (if any) by the government of the previous bonus issue.

The Revaluation reserve arises from the revaluation of fixed assets (mainly land and buildings purchased many years earlier). As this is in actuality an unrealised profit it is not available for distribution among shareholders.

Capital redemption reserves are amounts appropriated from profits to buy back capital such as redeemable preference shares.

Revenue reserves really represent the ploughback of profits and it is important to look at these as they show the commitment the shareholders have to the company's growth and expansion. If all the profits made are distributed to the shareholders as dividends, a time will come when the company would have no money to modernise, to replace the assets and to expand. A wise management would always ensure a large percentage of the profits are ploughed back. It really is "planning for a better tomorrow" and not the epicurian "tomorrow you may die".

Loans

Loans are divided into two—secured and unsecured. The secured loans are those that are secured to some or all the assets of the company. This means that at the time of dissolution or winding up the lender has the first right (before the others) to the proceeds from the sale of the assets. The usual secured loans are term loans for the purchase of machinery (against hypothecation of the specific machinery), working capital loans such as overdrafts (against the hypothecation of stocks and debentures) and debentures (against a floating charge of all the assets of the company.)

The notes are important as it also details the nature of loans the company has, the rate of interest payable and the date the loans are repayable. This allows a reader to calculate:

(a) The burden of interest the company has to bear,
(b) Whether it can easily pay the interest,
(c) Whether the loan repayment commitment can be met.

Unsecured loans are normally fixed deposits from the general public and short term loans from banks and financial institutions.

Fixed Assets

The Schedule of Fixed Assets breaks down fixed assets into its component parts such as land, buildings, plant and machinery and the likes and against the cost of each of these heads shows the balance brought forward, the purchases in the year, the disposals and the accumulated depreciation so that one is aware of the book value of the assets under each component head. In many cases, (especially if the company is old and had acquired its land many years earlier), the land is shown at a revalued cost. This is done usually to reflect current values so that shareholders and others would be aware of a company's current worth and not of a value that is tremendously understated.

The schedules and notes would also detail capital work in progress. This gives an indication of the plan the company has for expansion and growth.

Fixed assets also sometimes include heads of accounts such as goodwill that are not fixed assets at all. The Notes to Larsen & Toubro's and Reliance's Accounts have Rs. 729 lakhs and Rs. 123 lakhs respectively shown as goodwill. In an analysis these should be discounted as they have no tangible existence.

Investments

A company invests in companies it has a trade interest in or in other companies to utilise its surplus capital.

Trade investments are made to have an involvement in the affairs of either a supplier or a customer or in some cases a competitor. This usually helps the company manage its affairs better.

On September 30, 1986, Larsen & Toubro had the following trade investments.

112,500 shares of Rs. 100 each of Audio India Ltd.	Rs. 6.00 Lakhs.
4,250 shares of Rs. 1000 each of Tractors Engineers Ltd.	Rs. 30.00 Lakhs.
60,000 shares of Rs. 10 each of Tractors & Equipment Corporation Ltd.	Rs. 4.50 Lakhs.
	Rs. 40.50 Lakhs.

The other investments are usually in other companies, in cooperative building societies or in the units of the Unit Trust of India. The latter is usually the deployment of short term funds. In end 1985 Reliance Ltd had surplus cash and it had purchased units of the Unit Trust of India for Rs. 36.93 crores. They were all sold in 1986 when the funds had to be utilised elsewhere. Purchase of units are a safe and profitable way of investing funds. The other avenues of deployment are intercorporate loans or other advances but in these cases the funds are tied in for a certain period of time (90 days, 180 days etc.) There is an element of risk too in that the borrowing company may not be able to repay in time. To counteract this the rewards are normally high—about 20% p.a. whereas the return on units are around 12% p.a.

Current Assets

Current assets are those assets that are cash or assets that will convert to cash/cash equivalents within 12 months.

The first component of current assets that one should look at are stocks or inventories. These are broken down to raw materials, stock in process and finished goods. One must check whether stocks have grown especially finished goods because if it has it may mean that the company is having difficulty in selling its products. Similarly if raw materials have depleted enormously it could mean that the company is

49

experiencing difficulty in procuring raw materials and there may be a danger of fall in production or stoppage in the future. These are hints and must be looked at.

Stocks are normally valued at the lower of cost or market value. However, in some cases, there may be a change in practice to either increase or reduce profits and the reader must therefore check whether any of this has happened. Reliance's 1986 Accounts had the following notes:

"Until last year inventories were valued at cost. During the year the company changed the method of valuation of inventories and accordingly, these are valued at cost or market value whichever is the lower. Had the same method been used inventories and profit would have been higher by Rs. 5.10 crores."

This statement informs the reader that due to the company changing its accounting principles and valuing stock at the lower of cost or market value profits have fallen by Rs. 5.10 crores. More interestingly it poses a question—why is cost higher than the market value? If that is so is the company making only unprofitable items? What is being done to reverse this trend? These questions are not normally answered in the report but the wise reader would be advised to consider them in his evaluation of the company.

Debtors represent customers to whom the company has sold its products and from whom monies are due. They are sub-divided between those that are over 6 months and others and differentiated between good and doubtful.

Reliance's 1986 schedules detailed debtors in the following manner:

	1986	1985
	(Rs. in crores)	
Over 6 months considered good	17.22	8.86
Considered doubtful	2.04	1.68
	19.26	10.54
Less: Provision/or doubtful debts	2.04	1.68
	17.22	8.86
Others considered good *)*	103.25	100.55
	120.47	109.41

The above indicates that the company had Rs. 2.04 crores of bad debts all of which were provided for.

Sometimes, the entire amount considered doubtful may not be provided for.

In DCM's Accounts for the year ended June 30, 1987 it was noted that it had the following amounts doubtful

Debts over six months	Rs. 1,64,64,419
Others	Rs. 2,22,152
	Rs. 1,66,86,571
Against this the provision was only	Rs. 7,50,000
	Rs. 1,59,36,571

Rs. 1.59 crores was not provided for. The analyst must adjust for this while evaluating the company.

Orkay's analysis of debtors was as follows:

	1987 Rupees	1986 Rupees
Debts outstanding for a period exceeding six months	8,23,66,436	4,96,08,409
Other debts	24,83,80,933	14,15,02,262
	33,07,47,369	19,11,10,671

It would be observed that debtors have nearly doubled and it poses the questions—

(a) Why has this occurred?
(b) Are they likely to be realised?
(c) How much of these are likely to be doubtful?

Normally these increases are a warning—a warning of the difficulties a company is having to sell its products and to realise amounts due to it.

Cash and bank balances are amounts of cash the company has in hand or at current or deposit accounts with banks. As there are usually non-interest bearing few companies have any appreciable balances.

Loan and advances represent amounts, loaned to employees and others and deposits with government, quasi-government and other bodies.

They are differentiated between those considered good and those considered doubtful. Those that are considered doubtful are usually provided for in full. If they are not, then at the time of analysing the company, additional provisions should be considered.

Current Liabilities & Provisions

Current liabilities are those liabilities that are due by the company within the next twelve months and include amounts due to trade creditors, advances from customers and interest due on loans and acceptances. It is important to check these. A large increase may suggest that the company is having difficulty in meeting its liabilities.

In Orkay's accounts to March 31, 1987, Current liabilities were as under:

	1987	1986
	\(Rs. in lakhs\)	
Sundry Creditors	2245	1384
Dividend warrants posted but not encashed	24	4
Interest accrued but not due	255	29
	2524	1417

There has been an enormous increase in nearly all the different components and suggests possible cash difficulties which should be investigated.

Provisions are amounts set aside for known liabilities and the usual provisions that a company have at the year end are for dividends and for tax.

Apart from schedules relating to the Balance Sheet, companies are required to submit details of income and expenditure.

Income

Income arises from two sources—from the sale of the company's products and from other income. The reader must go through the details of other income and examine its makeup as they may include items that are not income at all.

DCM's accounts for the year to June 30, 1987 included the following under other income—

	1987	1986
Excess provisions of previous years		
Written back	2,57,43,915	8,04,13,239
Others	2,75,60,081	42,14,605

Excess provisions written back is not really income but adjustments relating to previous years and should be shown as a prior year adjustment after the profit for the year has been arrived at.

Expenditure

The expenditure incurred in manufacturing the goods sold, repairs made, salaries and wages paid, administration and selling expenses and all other costs are detailed in the schedule of expenditure.

This is an extremely useful schedule as it enables one to examine the increase/decrease under the different heads of expenditure and to determine whether they are excessive.

Notes

The notes to the accounts are probably the most important feature in the financial statements as it is here that the company actually states its company policies and the changes that it has done and the liabilities that it has not provided before.

The most important liability the notes discuss is contingent liabilities. Contingent liabilities are those liabilities that may crystallise or become liabilities on the happening of an event which may or may not occur. The most common contingent liability that is seen on financial statements is for bills discounted. This is considered a contingent liability since should the customer refuse to pay, the liabilities would devolve on the company.

The notes are varied and include details of the makeup of items, changes in company policy and the likes. Reliance's 1986 statements include many different notes among which were—

(a) Sales in inclusive of Rs. 25.62 crores being the recovery of sales tax and excise duty;

(b) The company has been providing liability for excise duty in respect of finished products lying in factory premises/bond as and when they are removed on the understanding that duty becomes payable only at the time of removal of goods. Accordingly, estimated liability amounting to Rs. 61.06 crores in respect of such products at year end has not been provided in the accounts.

(c) The company until last year used to account for disposal of waste generated in the course of productions on cash basis. During the year one of the waste recovery plants was commissioned for recycling of polyester yarn and fibre waste as raw material. Had this not been done, the figures of raw materials consumption would have been higher by Rs. 11.72 crores and correspondingly, the profits for the year could have been lower by the said amount.

Particulars of capacity and production

Companies are required to detail particulars of their licenced and installed capacity against which it would show its production. These are broken down to the various products a company makes and as a consequence one is able to see at a glance how effectively the company is using its installed capacity.

Particulars of stocks and sales

A company is also required to detail the various stocks it holds of various products (opening and closing) and the sales made during the year. It gives the reader the opportunity to find out whether some items are slow moving and if others are being sold as fast as they are produced.

In short the Notes and Schedules to the accounts provide a wealth of information to a reader and it is not possible for a reader or analyst to evaluate a company without actually reading and assimilating the notes and schedules to the accounts.

PART II

PART II

4

RATIO ANALYSIS

Financial statements can be daunting. Most persons find them overwhelming even frightening purely because they do not understand them. As a result, they look at the net income and if it has increased look no further in the belief that all is well. This may not be true. Dividends may be being paid out of accumulated profits. The profitability may have decreased. The company's liquidity may have declined.

It is in the analysis of financial statements that ratios come into their own. They help —

★ to analyse the performance of a company and compare it with that of other similar companies.
★ to determine the relative weaknesses and strengths of a company.

Ratios put figures into perspective. It is difficult to see how a company is doing by looking at a large number of figures. Ratios summarise the figures in a form that is easily understood, interpreted and used.

The ratios described below would enable one to assess strengths and identify weaknesses, determine trends and forecast future performance.

Ratio analysis is an important management tool and its skilful use and action taken based on interpretations made can make a company grow from strength to strength.

MARGINS

Margins indicate returns or earnings on sales. They are useful in:

1. Characterising the cost structures of businesses.
2. Comparing performance between companies within an industry.
3. Assessing trends in managements performance.

(a) **Gross Margin**

This shows profitability or mark-up on goods sold.

$$\frac{\text{Sales-cost of goods sold}}{\text{Sales}}$$

(b) **Operating margin**

Operating Margin indicates the profitability of a company before the cost of financing, tax and and other miscellaneous income.

$$\frac{\text{Operating profit}}{\text{Sales}}$$

(c) **Breakeven margin**

The ratio indicates the number of items that need to be sold to meet fixed costs.

$$\frac{\text{Fixed costs}}{\text{Sales-cost of goods sold/no. of items sold.}}$$

(d) **Prefinancing margin**

The prefinancing margin shows rate of profit earned on sales prior to the cost of finance

$$\frac{\text{Earning before interest \& tax}}{\text{Sales}}$$

(e) **Pretax margin**

This is calculated to determine the rate earned on sales after the cost of financing but before tax.

$$\frac{\text{Pretax Income}}{\text{Sales}}$$

(f) **Net Profit Margin**

The net profit margin indicates rate of earnings a company makes after tax on sales.

$$\frac{\text{Net income after tax}}{\text{Sales}}$$

PROFITABILITY

Profitability ratios indicate a company's profitability—

   (i) in relation to other companies within the industry.
  (ii) to previous years
                    and
 (iii) show the management's effectiveness as shown by returns generated on sales and investments.

58

(a) Return on total assets (ROTA)

$$\frac{\text{Net Income after Tax}}{\text{Average Total assets.}}$$

The return on total assets ratio allows one to examine whether:

   (i) margin on sales earned is reasonable

   (ii) assets of the company are adequately and effectively used

   (iii) the interest payments made by the company are too high

(b) Return on equity

$$\frac{\text{Net Income after tax less dividend on preference shares}}{\text{Average share holder's equity.}}$$

This measures whether the return on shareholders' investments is better than other alternatives available.

(c) Return on total invested Capital

$$\frac{\text{Earnings before interest and tax}}{\text{Average total invested capital}}$$

This ratio enables one to examine whether the return earned is in excess of that earned elsewhere. Invested capital includes shareholders' funds and loans.

LIQUIDITY

Liquidity ratios help one to ascertain whether a company can pay its currently maturing financial obligations (payment of interest etc.) as well as have enough cash to meet its operational requirements.

(a) Current Ratio

$$\frac{\text{Current assets}}{\text{Current Liabilities.}}$$

This is the most common measure of liquidity and is used to check whether the company has adequate current assets to meet its current liabilities.

59

(b) Quick or acid test

This is applied to examine whether a company has adequate cash or cash equivalents to meet its current obligations without having to resort to liquidating non-cash assets.

$$\frac{\text{Cash \& cash equivalents}}{\text{Current Liabilities.}}$$

DEBT SERVICE CAPACITY

Debt service capacity ratios are calculated to check whether a company can service its debts i.e. generate enough profits to be able to pay the interest and principal repayment on loans given:

(a) Debt coverage ratio

This ratio indicates the period it would take for a company to pay its short and long term debt from internally generated funds or profits.

$$\frac{\text{Net profit after tax + Depreciation}}{\text{Average Loans.}}$$

(b) Interest coverage

Interest coverage ratio measures whether a company has adequate profits to meet the interest payments on its obligations.

$$\frac{\text{Earnings before interest and tax}}{\text{Interest expense.}}$$

(c) Fixed charge coverage

This ratio considers whether the company makes sufficient income before interest and rental expenses to meet its interest and rental obligations.

$$\frac{\text{Earnings before interest \& tax rental expenses}}{\text{Interest + rental expenses.}}$$

ASSET MANAGEMENT/EFFICIENCY

Asset management or efficiency ratios are calculated to

consider how effectively a company is managing its assets. These ratios can be used to assess trends and are very useful in making financial statement forecasts.

(a) **Stock utilization or turnover**

$$\frac{\text{Cost of good sold}}{\text{Average Stocks}}$$

This measures the times stocks have turned over in a year or the number of days stocks are held to support sales. This enables one to check whether the company holds excessive stock.

OR

$$\frac{365 \times \text{Average Stocks}}{\text{Cost of goods sold}}$$

(b) **Average collection period**

This ratio represents the length of time a company must wait after making a sale before it actually receives cash from its customers. This ratio is important in assessing the effectiveness of the credit administration of the company.

$$\frac{\text{Average trade debtors} \times 365 \text{ days}}{\text{Sales}}$$

(c) **Total Asset utilisation**

$$\frac{\text{Sales}}{\text{Average total assets}}$$

The total asset utilisation ratio is calculated to check whether a company is generating a sufficient volume of business taking into consideration the size of its asset investment.

LEVERAGE/COVERAGE

Leverage measures the extent assets are covered by liabilities and the extent loans and liabilities are a source of funds. Companies with a high leverage can afford less reduction in asset values at the time of liquidation.

(a) **Liabilities/Asset**

$$\frac{\text{Total Liabilities}}{\text{Total Assets}}$$

This ratio indicates the total funds provided by creditors to the business.

(b) Debt/Net worth

The debt/net worth ratio indicates the extent a company is financed by borrowed funds.

$$\frac{\text{Loans}}{\text{Share Capital + Reserves}}$$

(c) Liabilities/Net Worth

This ratio measures the extent a company is financed by liabilities.

$$\frac{\text{Total Liabilities}}{\text{Share Capital + Reserves}}$$

EARNINGS

The earnings ratios indicate the earnings per common share and provides a measure whereby the performance of a company can be compared with others.

(a) Earnings per share

This ratio indicates the earnings attributable to a share.

$$\frac{\text{Income after tax and preference dividend}}{\text{Weighted average number of ordinary shares}}$$

(b) Dividend payout

The dividend payout ratio shows the amount of dividend paid out of earnings.

$$\frac{\text{Dividend}}{\text{Net Income after tax}}$$

(c) Price earnings

The price earnings ratio or P/E ratio shows how long it would take to recover the cost of investment.

$$\frac{\text{Market Value}}{\text{Dividend paid}}$$

5

CASH FLOW AND LIQUIDITY

This is the age of creative accounting and innovative ideas. Accounting principles are changed, provisions are manipulated and accounting theory itself is engineered by companies to create profits sometimes out of thin air. Shareholders and investors are generally a gullible lot and look no further than the published figures. It comes to them as a surprise therefore when a company that had been declaring profits and paying dividends suddenly downs its shutters and goes out of business. What happened? They ask themselves. How could this be? The reason usually lies in the fact that the company has no cash and could not pay its creditors. This is an area that is not often considered—the company's cashflow and yet it is for a company its very lifeblood. This fact has always been recognised by the premier trading community of India—the Marwaris and they deal entirely on cash inflows and outflows. This is their strength and the reason for their growth.

Stirling Homex was one of the major construction companies in the United States. Its growth was phenomenal. And yet, at its prime, it filed for bankruptcy under Chapter II. The reason was that it had no money to pay its creditors. Nearer home, Nirlon Ltd., an excellent, well reputed company ran into difficulties on account of its inability to raise working capital and pay its creditors.

It is imperative to realise that Balance Sheets can be windowdressed and profits can, with ingenuity, be whatever one wants it to be. It is not however possible to manipulate the cashflow of a company—its sources and uses of funds— and it is important that at the time of evaluation, the reader examines a company's sources and uses of funds. Its importance has already been recognised in the United States where it is mandatory for a company to publish with its

Annual Report a statement of changes in financial statements which is in effect a cashflow statement.

A sources & uses statement begins with the profit for the year to which are added the increases in liability accounts (sources) and from which are reduced the increases in asset accounts (uses). The net result shows whether there has been an excess or deficit of funds and how this was financed.

Reliance Industries Ltd. published a profit of Rs. 14.17 crores in the year to December 31, 1986. It was a fall from its previous years results of Rs. 71.34 crores but still it was a good result in hard times. Reliance is one of the industries too which has been accused of having no money as a consequence of which it has been converting its debentures to equity shares.

Reliance's Balance Sheet is shown on exhibit I (page 68) and based on this its sources and uses of funds are shown on exhibit II (page 69).

It would be noticed that although from its operations, the company was able to raise Rs. 75.15 crores it was entirely used in the raising of working capital. It effectively paid its dividends from borrowed funds. It also poses the question that when the time comes to repay the loans, will the company have adequate monies to do so? This company is frequently raising monies from the general public in the form of rights shares and convertible debentures. It is important to remember that this has to be serviced and can create enormous problems.

Orkay Silk Mills shares were a few years ago quoting at around Rs. 200 a share. Rumours came into the market of the company being unable to meet its debt obligations; of there being the siphoning of cash out and the shares fell and fell to reach a price of around Rs. 21 in December 1987.

The balance sheet and sources and uses of funds statements are shown as exhibits III & IV respectively (Pages 70 & 71).

It would be noted that the company did have a positive operating cash flow. However it had an enormous investment in fixed assets in the year which was partly financed by the issue of share capital and by the increase in loans. In this situation it is important to consider whether the company would be able to repay the loans that it has taken especially when it is more than its share capital and especially so if it is in a cyclical industry like the textile industry.

In short the importance of the sources and uses of funds can not be over emphasised as it reveals exactly from where the monies come for a company and how it has been utilised.

A reader must also check how liquid a company is i.e. whether it can discharge its currently maturing financial obligations as well as have enough cash to meet its operational requirements. If a company cannot do so, it may be forced to sell its more important assets at a loss and, in extreme cases be forced into liquidation.

The most common measure of liquidity is the current ratio. This is computed by dividing current assets by current liabilities. As a general rule, the safe factor is 2:1 which means that current assets should be double current liabilities. A decrease between one year and the next should create queries as a fall in liquidity can create enormous difficulties.

In the examples shown in exhibits I & III it would be observed that Reliance's current ratio fell from 2.91:1 in 1985 to 1.05:1 in 1986. Similarly Orkay's fell from 2.85:1 in 1986 to 2.28:1 in 1987 Reliance's is worrying especially when this is looked at together with a deficit cash flow.

The other test for liquidity is the quick or acid test which is applied to examine whether a company has adequate cash or cash equivalents to meet its current obligations without having to resort to liquidating non cash. assets such as stocks. This ratio aims to emphasise that the immediate sale of stocks would be less than at cost. Hence it checks whether the company has adequate cash or easily realisable assets.

This ratio is calculated by dividing cash and easily saleable investments and debtors by current liabilities. Orkay had.a quick ratio of 1.08:1 in 1986 and 1.18:1 in 1987 (an improvement). This means that Orkay had adequate funds in cash or near cash items to payoff all current liabilities. Reliance's on the other hand is the reverse. In 1985 it had a quick ratio of 2.32:1 which was excellent but this fell to 0.90:1 in 1986 which means that it does not have sufficient funds to meet its obligations with readily available cash.

The defensive ratio is used to indicate the number of days a company can theoretically remain in business without additional sales or new loans. This is calculated by dividing the average daily cash expenditures for operating expenses by the company's most liquid assets. In the calculation of this ratio the liquid assets consist of only cash or cash equivalents. Debtors and stocks are not considered as they are not the equivalent of cash. A ratio of 0.05 indicates that a company can continue business without liquidating its assets for 20 days.

The current liability coverage ratio, though of limited value, examines the relationship of cash-in-flow (funds from operations—see exhibits II & IV) and current liabilities. This ratio indicates whether the company can meet its currently maturing liabilities from internally generated funds.

In regard to Orkay and Reliance its details are as follows:

	Orkay	Reliance
Funds from Operation	11.28	75.15
Current Liabilities	29.25	1001.23
Current Liabilities coverage	0.38	0.075

In the case of Orkay it means that funds from operations are only 38% of the current liabilities of the company and if these liabilities are to be paid out of funds from operations, it would take 2.6 years to do so. It would not be totally correct to take Reliance's ratio as its liabilities include monies that have to be returned to those who applied for the company's 'G' series debentures.

It should be noted that as a company begins to experience financial difficulties, it pays its bills more slowly. This results in the building up of current liabilities. If current liabilities are rising faster than the building up of current assets, it could result in the company facing financial trouble and being unable to meet its obligations. Hence a deterioration in the current ratio should cause concern.

However, a negative current ratio need not necessarily be bad. Many concerns that have very high stock turnovers and sell for cash normally have more current liabilities than current assets. This also does not mean that these concerns are liquid. It is not possible therefore to generalise on the ideal ratio. Liquidity ratios will vary from industry to industry and from company to company.

It must be remembered too that companies before they actually "crash" become more liquid. This occurs as inventories and fixed assets are sold and become converted into cash. At the same time current liabilities reduce as creditors are paid off.

Liquidity ratios are susceptible to window dressing, companies have been known to sell at the year end, stocks at depressed prices in order to show greater liquidity. It is important, therefore, to see the trends.

A large current ratio is not necessarily good. It may be due to an increase in stocks—stocks which the company is unable to sell. It may be due too to inefficiency in the control of assets. Debtor collection may be weak. Or the company may have too much cash in its year end—cash that it is unable to invest due to a lack of attractive opportunities.

Liquidity should be at optimum levels rather than at highest levels. The optimum level will change, however, from company to company and industry to industry.

The reader will be wise to examine the company's cash flow and its liquidity as it would indicate the financial viability of the company and these statements do, in reality, tear the curtains down and reveal the stark and naked truth. And this is what one needs to know.

EXHIBIT 'I'

Reliance Industries Ltd.

(Rs. in crores)

| | Balance At 31st Dec. | | Movement |
	1986	1985	1986
Assets			
Fixed Assets	949.46	606.80	342.66
Investments	0.37	37.30	(36.93)
Current Assets	1052.83	402.10	650.73
	2002.66	1046.20	956.46
Shareholders funds			
Equity Share Capital	51.61	51.61	—
Preference Share Capital	5.80	5.80	—
Reserves & Surplus	254.12	253.71	0.41
	311.53	311.12	0.41
Liabilities			
Long term funds	546.12	515.16	30.96
Medium/Short Term funds	143.78	81.90	61.88
Current Liabilities	1001.23	138.02	863.21
	1691.13	735.08	956.05
Total Shareholders Funds + Liabilities	2002.66	1046.20	956.46

EXHIBIT 'II'

Reliance Industries Ltd.

Sources and Uses of Funds for the Year to December 31, 1986

(Rs. in Crores)

Sources	
Operating net income for the year	14.17
Non cash items depreciation	60.98
Funds from Operation	75.15
Increase in trade creditors	18.11
Increase in provisions	0.31
Increase in stocks	(92.74)
Increase in debtors (trade)	(10.93)
Increase in other debtors	(14.16)
Operating cash flow	(24.26)
Disposals of fixed assets	0.24
Sale of units of the Unit Trust of India	36.93
Increase in creditor for capital expenditure	67.12
	80.03
Uses	
Purchase of fixed assets	403.88
Dividends paid	25.75
	429.63
Excess (deficit)	(349.60)
Financed by	
Increase in loans	190.17
Application monies received	692.33
Increase in Bank balances	(532.66)
Increase in cash	(0.24)
	349.60

EXHIBIT 'III'

ORKAY SILK MILLS LIMITED.

(Rs. in lakhs)

	At March 31, 1987	1986	Movement
Source			
Shareholders' Funds	6896	4125	2771
Loan Funds	8640	6460	2180
	15536	10585	4951
APPLICATION OF FUNDS			
Net fixed assets	11755	6836	4919
Investments	13		13
Current Assets	6693	5773	920
	18461	12609	5852
Less Current Liabilities	2925	2024	901
	15536	10585	4951
Current Ratio	2.28	2.85	
Quick Ratio	1.18	1.08	

EXHIBIT 'IV'

ORKAY SILK MILLS LTD

Sources and uses of Funds at March 31, 1987

(Rs. in lakhs)

SOURCES	
Operating net income for the year	784
Non cash items	
Depreciation for current year	344
Funds from operations	1128
Reduction in Stocks	447
Increase in current liabilities	1107
Increase in debtors	(1396)
Increase in loans & advances	(102)
Payment of tax	(125)
Operating cash flow	1059
Sale of fixed assets	235
Extraordinary items & prior year adjustments	420
Total Sources	**1714**

USES	
Additions of fixed assets	5498
Purchases of units of the Unit Trust of India	13
Payment of dividend	404
	5915
Excess (deficit)	(4201)

Financed by	
Issue of share capital	1890
Increase in loans	2180
Decrease in balances at banks	131
	4201

6

LEVERAGE & STABLE LEVERAGED GROWTH

A company purchases assets and funds its working capital with equity (shareholders' funds) and by borrowing from banks and financial institutions. The ratio of finance raised between shareholders funds and borrowed funds is of critical importance to the company's profitability and growth.

Companies that are highly leveraged (or geared as this is sometimes termed) are those that are very dependant on borrowed funds. These companies can afford less reduction in asset values at the time of liquidation.

In a highly leveraged company profits will be high during the boom years—the years of growth. The return to shareholders will be large. However, in bad years the reverse would occur. The earnings may entirely be utilised to pay the interest on borrowings and there may not be any return to the ordinary shareholders at all. The effect of leverage on companies is illustrated below:

	Company X Rs. in lakhs	Company Y Rs. in lakhs	Company Z Rs. in lakhs
Balance Sheet Excerpt			
Share capital	1000	9000	10.000
Borrowed funds @ 15% p.a.	9000	1000	—
	10,000	10,000	10.000
Good Year			
Earning before interest & tax	3000	3000	3000
Interest paid @ 15% p.a.	1350	150	—
	1650	2850	3000
Tax @ 60%	990	1710	1800
	660	1140	1200

	Company X Rs. in lakhs	Company Y Rs. in lakhs	Company Z Rs. in lakhs
Return to equity shareholders			
(i) before tax %	165.0	31.7	30.0
(ii) after tax %	66.0	12.7	12.0
Reasonable year			
Earning before Interest & tax	1800	1800	1800
Interest paid @ 15% p.a.	1350	150	—
	450	1650	1800
Tax @ 60%	270	990	1080
	180	660	720
Return to equity shareholders			
(i) before tax %	45.0	18.3	18.0
(ii) after tax %	18.0	7.3	7.2
Bad Year			
Earnings before Interest & tax	1350	1350	1350
Interest @ 15% p.a.	1350	150	—
	—	1200	1350
Tax @ 60%	Nil	720	810
	—	480	540
Return to equity shareholders			
(i) before tax %	—	13.3	13.5
(ii) after tax %	—	5.3	5.4

It is apparent from the above illustration that in the years of growth—of boom, the highly leveraged company is the most profitable. This is true as long as the return or the rate of profit is more than the cost of borrowed funds. However, should there be a reversal—should recession set in, the profits of highly leveraged companies would be used to service the borrowings made and there would be hardly anything left for the ordinary shareholders.

It may be stated that companies that have low debt stand a greater chance of survival when the economy or the industry is at a recession. They have to expect, for this safety, much lower returns at a time of boom. Conversely a highly leveraged company bears a high risk of losses at a depression or recession and the chance or opportunity of large profits in a boom.

It is important at the time of reading an Annual report to look at its leverage and whether the company can service its capital. Inability to do so can mean its death. Nirlon was till recently a wellknown and well reputed company. It was involved in various expansion and diversification programmes but due to illfortunes, it could not service its debts and the result was that the company came to its knees. Similar problems are being faced by Star Textiles and others.

In order to assess leverage, a reader could evaluate risks by calculating the following leverage ratios.

Please peruse exhibit I on page 80. The Balance Sheet of Orkay Silk Mills Ltd has been chosen to illustrate the ratios.

Liabilities to Assets Ratio

The liabilities to assets ratio is a pure measure of asset coverage and indicates the total funds provided by creditors to the business i.e. the extent the company is financed by out-siders (persons other than shareholders). Liabilities in this connection includes both current and long term assets. Assets, on the other hand, are total assets, less intangible assets such as good-will and deferred assets.

The relevant details of Orkay are as follows:

	1987	1986
Total Assets	18461	12601
Less: Goodwill	3	3
	18458	12598
Total Liabilities		
Loan funds	8640	6460
Current Liabilities	2925	2024
The Liabilities to assets ratio would be	$\dfrac{11565}{18458} = 62.7\%$	$\dfrac{8484}{12598} = 67.3\%$

Orkay became less leveraged in 1987 on account of an issue of shares which widened the equity base and increased shareholders funds.

A ratio of 62.7% in 1987 means that the company can sell its assets even at 63% of its book value and still meet its commitments. Conversely it could be said that the company can meet its commitments by selling 63% of its assets.

Debt/Asset Ratio

This ratio attempts to measure how well debt or borrowed funds are covered by assets and tries to determine the extent assets can depreciate in value before the company would cease being able to meet its commitments in regard to borrowings made.

Orkay's loan funds were Rs. 8640 lakhs and Rs. 6460 lakhs in 1987 and 1986 respectively whereas its total tangible assets were Rs. 18458 lakhs and Rs. 12598 lakhs. Its debt/assets ratio would be

1987	46.8%
1986	51.2%

Orkay's ratios have improved and it indicates that the assets must fall in value by nearly 54% before the company ceases to be able to meet its commitments.

Debt/Net Worth Ratio

The debt to net worth ratio indicates the extent a company is financed by borrowed funds. In the calculation of net worth, goodwill and other intangibles are deducted:

	1987 Rs. in lakhs	1986 Rs. in lakhs
Net Worth		
Shareholders funds	6896	4125
Less: Goodwill	3	3
	6893	4122
Loan funds	8640	6460
Ratio	1.25 times	1.56 times

This means that borrowed funds are 1.25 times more than the shareholders' equity and that for every Rs.1.25 borrowed, the shareholders commitment is only Re. 1.00.

Liabilities/Net Worth

The liabilities to net worth ratio measures the extent a company is financed by liabilities. As it includes all the liabilities in its computation it is a more indicative ratio than the debt to net worth ratio.

Orkay's details are as follows:

	1987 Rs. lakhs	1986 Rs. lakhs
Total liabilities	11565	8484
Net Worth	6893	4122
The ratio is therefore	1.68	2.05

The ratio is more realistic as, at the time a company is liquidated, all liabilities need to be considered whether interest bearing or otherwise. Liabilities are 1.6 times shareholders funds. Total liabilities also account for 62% of all the assets which means that 62% of the assets are financed by outside borrowings.

At the time of going through the annual report one should also examine contingent liabilities such as law suits, guarantees and claims against the company as the possibility arises of their crystallising and should they do so—it could have a material bearing on the company's leverage. A prime example is that of ITC which has an excise claim of over Rs. 800 crores. The company is disputing it but should it be established that the company does owe the government this—the company's entire net worth would be wiped out.

Creditors and investors normally prefer low leverage ratios since the lower the ratio, the greater the cushion against losses in the event of a liquidation or a fall in demand and low profits. On the other hand, owners may prefer high leverage ratios to magnify earnings or to keep their equity low to keep control of the company.

In short leverage ratios indicate whether a company has over borrowed, whether it has the capacity to obtain additional funds and the effects on the profits of leverage. The importance of leverage is appreciated when it is realised that if a company during a period of growth borrows extensively, it can collapse should a recession occur and sales and profits fall.

Stable Leveraged growth

Companies have to grow and when companies grow it has to have larger working capital and other assets. To finance these companies either issue more capital or borrow more. The questions that can arise are—

(a) Whether the rate of growth is very rapid. If it is, the possibility exists that the company may not be able to create or build an infrastructure to support this growth.

(b) Whether the company has borrowed more than it should.

While the former problem can be surmounted by planning, it is the latter that causes concern.

As a company grows, its level of operations increases and to support this level it needs to keep larger stocks. So stocks increase. As sales grow and credit is extended to support and boost sales, amounts due from customers (debtors) will rise. Purchase too will increase. In short all those assets that are directly involved with or support sales will increase such as stocks, debtors and creditors. These are known as net working investments.

In order to consider stable leveraged growth one has to consider the ratio or relationship net working investments normally have to sales. The means the net working investments required to support sales at a level. If the sales of a company is Rs. 100 crores and its net working investments are Rs. 20 crores it would have a net working investments/sales ratio of 0.2%. The company requires therefore for every Rs. 100/- of sales Rs. 20 of net working investments. If in the next year the company's sale increases by 40%, its net working investments should increase by 40% to maintain the equilibrium. This increase in net working investments would need to be financed by borrowings and normally as the cost of funds are high the net income earned by the company would be less.

At a time of growth the question would arise as the kind of financing that should be taken. If this financing is by the issue of equity there is no problem as no interest has to be paid and the capital base is strengthened. It would be a different if the growth is financed by loans. Interest would need to be paid. Principal would need to be repaid. At a time of growth there would be no real problem. However, problems would arise should the situation change and recession set in as during this time there will be a fall in demand and in sales. This would lead to a build up of stocks that would need to be financed. Interest and capital repayments would have to be paid. The result could lead to losses and more losses.

The effect of this is best described in the following example—

	Normal growth Year 1 Rs.	Growth at 40% Year 2 Rs.	Fall in demand Year 3 Rs.
Income Statement			
Sales	1000	1400	1200
Earning before interest and tax	200	240	180
Interest	100	104	110
Pretax income	100	136	70
Tax @ 40%	40	56	30
Net Income	60	80	40
Balance Sheet			
Cash	20	20	20
Net working investments	300	420	480
Fixed assets	80	90	90
Loans	200	250	270
Shareholders funds	200	280	320

It would be observed that while the company is growing it is able to maintain its margins and profits in spite of increase in loans by 25%. However when there is a fall in sales as a result of a fall in demand the company is not able to sell its stocks and debtors take longer to pay. The company is

78

forced to borrow more to finance this. The consequence is lower profits.

A fall in demand is not the sole reason for a company's profitability to decline. A company may expand very rapidly and to assist this growth the company may be extending credit for longer periods and building up stocks. If in order to do this, heavy borrowings are made and margins are low, the cash flow can be negative and eventually the company may suffer losses.

The growth of a company should therefore be at a rate that its leverage can sustain the growth rate. At this rate the net increase in borrowings is equal to the increase in income after tax but before dividend. Adjustments should be made to maintain this level by issuing shares. If this ratio—the stable leverage growth ratio—is maintained a company can grow without fear for its financial future.

EXHIBIT 'I'

ORKAY SILK MILLS LIMITED

BALANCE SHEET AS AT 31 st MARCH 1987.

(Rs. in lakhs)

		1987	1986
SOURCE OF FUNDS			
Shareholders funds			
Capital		2403	1615
Reserve & Surplus		4493	2510
		6896	4125
Loan funds			
Secured		6664	4841
Unsecured		1976	1619
		8640	6460
	TOTAL ...	15536	10585
APPLICATION OF FUNDS			
Fixed assets		11755	6836
Investments		13	—
Current Assets		6693	5773
		18461	12609
Less: Current Liabilities		2925	2024
		15536	10585
Included in above			
(i) Goodwill in fixed assets		3	3
Current assets include			
Stocks		2673	3120
Debtors (trade)		3307	1911
Current Liabilities include			
Trade Creditors		2245	1384

7

DEBT SERVICE CAPACITY

In mid 1987 there was a rumour that Orkay Silk Mills Ltd. had defaulted on a foreign currency loan that it had taken. Nirlon has been going through a very difficult phase and has been having difficulty in servicing its borrowings. Star Textiles has not paid the interest on its debentures for some time and it had sent a circular to its members and debenture holders that it is attempting to enter into an arrangement with the financial institutions which would rejuvenate the company. Punjab Anand cannot service its debts. Those who had lent to WG Forge are unlikely to receive their monies back in the forseeable future. These and many other well known companies have had trying times to service their debts. Some such as Star Textiles and WG Forge have become sick.

How did this come about? The reasons are diverse. The major and usual reason has been that they had borrowed heavily during the boom years of their growth and were unable to service these borrowings when demand for their products fell. Another reason is that monies had been borrowed at a high rate of interest—a rate that became uneconomical when due to competition margins had to be reduced. Whatever be the reason it is finally the lender (the debenture holder, banks etc.) and ultimately the share holder that suffers because it is they who finally stand to lose their stake.

It is important therefore that prior to purchasing debentures in a company or placing fixed deposits in it or even purchasing shares in the company that one checks whether the company can service its debts. A company that cannot generate adequate profits to meet its debt commitments is a company on the verge of collapse.

A company's ability to service debts can be assessed by examining its debt service capacity ratios. The basic assumption in these ratios is that a company is a going concern and that the debts would be repaid out of internally generated funds and not from the sale of assets or from additional borrowings. The debt service ratios therefore indicate the relationship between cash flow (internally generated funds) and the company's liabilities.

THE DEBT COVERAGE RATIO

This ratio is calculated for find out the period it would take a company to repay its borrowings (loans) from internally generated funds or profits. It is an important ratio if loans are to be repaid from operating income and is of limited value if the repayment is to be from the sale of assets. Internally generated funds in this context is the net profit after tax to which is added non cash expenses such as depreciation. Loans or borrowings would include both secured and unsecured loans. The ratio is calculated by dividing internally generated funds by the average debt.

A ratio of 0.125 indicates that it would take a company 8 years to repay its borrowed funds (debts) from internally generated funds.

On perusing exhibit I (page 86) it would be observed that Orkay Silk Mills has a debt coverage ratio of 0.150 which means that Orkay has a capacity to repay its borrowings from internally generated funds in 6.7 years. Reliance on the other hand has a coverage of 0.1777 and DCM has a coverage of 0.264. DCM is obviously therefore the strongest as it can repay its debts in 3.8 years whereas Reliance would take 5-7 years to do so.

This ratio is relevant if a short term loan is to be extended which is to be repaid through internally generated funds.

LIABILITY COVERAGE RATIO

The liability coverage ratio is a more intense ratio as it attempts to determine the time it would take a company to pay off all its liabilities from internally generated funds. It presumes that liabilities would not be liquidated, as is often done, by additional borrowings or from the sale of assets.

The ratio is arrived at by dividing internally generated funds by the average total liabilities.

An extract from the financial statements of ITC Ltd. for the year ended 30th June 1987 are as follows:—

	Rs. in lakhs
Net Profit before tax	1586
Taxation (refund)	(158)
Profit after tax	1744
Depreciation on fixed Assets	695
Internally generated funds	2439

	1987 Rs. in lakhs	1986 Rs. in lakhs
Loans funds	12423	11154
Current Liabilities & Provisions	8723	5973
Total Liabilities	21146	17127

ITC's liability coverage ratio is 0.127 which means that ITC would take 7-8 years to pay its total liabilities.

This ratio is often calculated by considering as opposed to the average total liabilities, the total liabilities on the date of the Balance Sheet. This, it is argued, is more appropriate as the point that is to be determined is the time it would take to pay off the total liabilities at a particular time.

The liability coverage ratio is susceptible to window dressing as liabilities on the Balance Sheet date can be reduced by either paying them or by suppressing them.

INTEREST COVERAGE

This ratio is one of major importance as it measures whether a company has adequate profits to meet the interest payment on its loans. This ratio should be always considered before loans are being extended as the company may not be able to service it. The ratio is arrived at by dividing a company's earnings before interest and tax by its interest expense.

The relevant figures of DCM Ltd. and Hindustan Lever for the periods ended September 30, 1987 and December 31, 1986 were as follows:—

	D C M Ltd. Rs. lakhs	Hindustan Lever Rs. lakhs
Profit before tax	115	6507
Interest	2262	360
	2377	6867

DCM Ltd. has an interest coverage of just 1.05 times. It is just barely able to pay its interest. If demand falls or margins get squeezed it may find it very difficult to service its loans. On the other hand Hindustan Lever is extremely strong. Its earnings before interest and tax (EBIT) is 19 times its interest payments. It would have no difficulty in paying interest.

FIXED CHARGE COVERAGE

Money is at times, with various restrictions, difficult to procure. Companies may also not want to tie up their available cash in fixed assets but would want to utilise the available cash in working capital. As a consequence they may resort to what is known as off balance sheet financing. This means that the company instead of purchasing machinery or buildings etc. rent them or lease them. The rent paid being an operating expense is charged to the Profit and Loss Account.

The fixed charge coverage considers whether the company makes sufficient income before interest and rental expenses to meet its interest and legal obligations and shows the relationship between earnings and cost of debt and fixed charges. It is calculated by dividing earning before interest and tax and rental expenses by interest and rental expenses.

Larsen & Toubro's details of the above for the year ended September 30, 1986 was as follows:—

	Rs. lakhs
Profit before taxes	3142
Interest	3492
Rent	129
Hire of Plant & Machinery	185
	6948

Larsen & Toubro's fixed charge coverage is therefore 1.83 times. Larsen and Toubro does generate adequate income to pay its interest and rent expenses.

This ratio is a purer ratio than the interest coverage ratio as it considers the fixed obligations a company has and examines whether earnings are sufficient.

CASH FLOW SURPLUS RATIO

The cash flow surplus ratio presumes that in a going concern, investments will be made in capital assets and as a company grows so will its working capital. It suggests that a company's ability to service its debts should be considered only after increases in capital expenditure and working capital. In this context cash flow surplus is net profit after tax plus non cash charges less capital expenditure and increase in working capital. The ratio is calculated by dividing the cash surplus by the total average debt.

The average debt of XYZ Ltd. was Rs. 8500 lakhs. Its internally generated funds were Rs. 350 lakhs. In the year working capital had increased by Rs. 50 lakhs and capital expenditure of Rs. 100 lakhs had been incurred. XYZ's cash flow surplus ratio is 0.233. According to this, the company would take 42 years to repay its cash flows surplus.

It should be mentioned that this ratio is not commonly used. This is because, as a company grows, its increase in working capital and its fixed assets are usually financed by loans or the issue of fresh capital as their requirements are far more than which can be generated through its internally generated funds.

The debt service ratios had not been given the importance that was justly its due but it is now being accepted and recognised as being of great value. It is of interest to all—the debenture holder, the creditor, the bank and to every one else who has at some time the need to lend to a company to determine whether a company has the capacity/ability to service its debts and repay its liabilities. Companies whose earnings before interest and tax are equal or less than the interest expense that it has to bear are risky to loan monies to, as the loan itself may become doubtful. Similarly if a company claims it can pay its debts from its own internal generation it should be able to demonstrate this.

EXHIBIT 'I'

EXTRACT OF PERTINENT DETAILS FROM SELECTED COMPANIES

	Orkay Silk Mills Year to March 31, 1987 Rs. in lakhs	Reliance Industries Year to Dec. 31, 1986 Rs. in lakhs	DCM Year to June 30, 1987 Rs. in lakhs
Net Profit after tax	785	1417	49
Depreciation	344	6098	1205
Internally generated Funds	1129	7515	1254
Interest	527	5424	2262
	1656	12939	3516
Average Debt	7550	73073	13340

8

PROFITABILITY

A company is known by the profits it makes. Its profits reflect the quality of its products, the competence of its management and the efficiency of its organisation. Profits are indeed its very lifeblood. It is profits that makes the company grow; it is profits that attracts investors to it and it is profit that attract the finances required for expansion.

Profits are relative. A large company may have profits much larger than a smaller one but the smaller one may be better organised and more profitable. The submission made is that one should not look at mere numbers because the numbers can be misleading. What one must examine is the profit-ability—the returns earned on capital invested and the margins as this really differentiates the efficient from the inefficient—the good from the bad.

The profitability of companies can be evaluated by the use of margin ratios and return ratios.

Margin ratios

Margins indicate the return a company makes on sales. They are helpful in:

(a) Determining the cost structures of business
(b) Company performance between companies within an industry.
(c) Assessing trends.

By examining margins one can find out whether the increases on account of increases in raw materials and other expenses are being promptly passed onto customers or whether they are being absorbed by the company. Normally, if there is great demand for the company's products all increases would be promptly passed on. On the other hand when there is competition and only average demand a portion of cost increases is usually borne by the company. This is why in many annual reports one comes across the statement "there was increasing pressure on margin".

Some products are sold at a high markup whereas others are sold at a smaller one. If the product mix is good i.e. more of the higher marked up products are sold the margins would show an improvement. Similarly a low margin may be on account of a bad products mix.

It is important that margins be examined as they give a tremendous insight into the company's workings, demand for its products and its efficiency.

Gross Margin

The gross margin shows as a percentage the mark up or value added over the cost—the excess added to meet the selling general and administrative expenses of a company and to provide a return on the capital invested by the shareholders. The gross margin is arrived at by expressing the difference between the sales made and the cost as a percentage of sales.

An extract of Indian Rayons financial statements for the year ended June 30, 1987.

	1987 Rs. lakhs	1986 Rs. lakhs
Sales		
Sales	19976	18326
Less Excise duty	(2685)	(2490)
	17291	15836
Cost of Sales		
Decrease in stocks	116	201
Consumption of raw materials	6020	5429
Consumption of stores	1816	1633
Power & Fuel	2963	2411
	10915	9674
Gross Profit	6376	6162
Gross Margin	36.9	38.9

The company's margins have fallen by 2%. The reader must ascertain the reasons for this as it is material in the evaluation of the company. The reasons are often mentioned in the Annual Report. In Indian Rayon's Directors' Report it was stated "Operating results, however, were less encouraging largely, because of the demand recession in rayon yarn and cement as well as the uncontrollable rise in the cost of inputs, without a commensurate increase in sales realisation." Similarly it was stated in Reliance Industries' Directors' Report for the year to December 31, 1986 that, "there was a pressure on margins partly because of unrestricted smuggling of Polyester Fabrics as well as unrestricted imports of Polyester staple fibre and yarn and partly due to the higher levy on purified terephthalic acid (PTA) compared to dimethyl terephthalate (DMT) though both are alternative raw materials of the Polyester Industry and PTA being a superior raw material for the Polyester Industry. But for these factors, the gross profit would have smartly risen in consonance with the turnover."

On observing a fall in the gross margin the reader must ascertain or attempt to ascertain the reason for the fall. The fall could apart from cost increases have been due to reasons such as —

(a) In order to increase sales the company has purposely had a smaller mark up.
(b) On account of increased competition, the margins have been reduced to keep sales up.
(c) The gross margin has reduced due to the mix of sales being bad i.e. more lower profit bearing products being sold.

It should not be assumed, on finding that the gross margin has reduced that the company is becoming less profitable. It could be the consequence of a conscious and calculated decision to increase sales. Similarly an increase in gross margins may be on account of a price increase and may also show a fall in sales volume. In short, variations in the gross margin should be investigated before a conclusion is arrived at on the company.

Prefinancing Margin

The Prefinancing margin is the rate of profit earned on sales prior to the cost of finance (interest on borrowings). It is arrived at by dividing a company's earning before interest and tax (EBIT) by sales and expressing the result as a percentage of sales. This is a better measure of profitability than the net profit to sales margin as the amount of interest paid by one company to another would vary and is dependent on the manner its sources of funds are constituted.

Orkay Silk Mills and Reliance Industries Ltd. are similar companies. The relevant figures of their Income statements are as follows:—

	Reliance Industries		Orkay Silk Mills	
	Year to December 31		Year to March 31	
	1986	1985	1987	1986
	Rs. lakhs	Rs. lakhs	Rs lakhs	Rs. lakhs
Sales	90402	73314	22767	24256
Profit before tax	1417	7134	785	765
Interest	5424	2445	527	675
Earning before interest & tax	6841	9579	1312	1440
Prefinancing Margin	7.57	13.07	5.76	5.94

The margins had fallen for both the companies although that of Reliance has fallen much more. Reliance's 1986 figures are more in line with industry averages. In 1985, it had made super profits on its products.

Breakeven Margin

The breakeven margin indicates the number of items a company should sell to meet its fixed costs. This is arrived at by dividing the fixed costs of a company by the gross profit (sales less cost of sales) earned on an item. Although for very large companies—especially multiproduct companies—it is very useful in examining the relative profitability of products and is very crucial in decision making when considering alternatives of whether to purchase an item or to make it.

In 1989 Nikhila Ltd., a company that manufactures widgets, sold 90,000 units at a total sales value of Rs. 920 lakhs. Its cost of sales was Rs. 736 lakhs. Its fixed expenses were Rs. 102 lakhs. Its breakeven margin would be:

Sales	Rs. 920 lakhs
Less cost of sales	Rs. 740 lakhs
Gross Profit	Rs. 180 lakhs
Gross Profit per item	Rs. 200
Breakeven margin	$\dfrac{\text{Rs. }10200000}{200} = 51,000$ items.

Nikhila Ltd. would have to sell 51000 widgets before it can make a profit and for every widget sold above 51000 the company would make a profit of Rs.200.

This, as a measure, is useful in comparing the profitability of similar companies.

It should be remembered that low margins are not necessarily bad. There are many large companies that cut prices to be more competitive and to increase sales. Very high sales businesses like wholesalers and supermarkets are usually low margin ones.

Margins may change due to changes in sales policies, sales price increases, cost increases and product mix changes. Therefore at all stages prior to making an opinion on the operating performance of the company, the reasons for the changes should be ascertained.

Profitability Ratios

Profitability ratios indicate—

(a) A company's profitability in relation to other companies within the industry.
(b) A company's profitability in relation to previous years.
(c) The management's effectiveness.

The ratio should be considered in consonance with rates of inflation and the cost of capital and borrowings. Trends in ratios are indicators of future development.

As the income of a company is earned over a period of time, the ratios should be calculated whenever possible on average asset and liability figures.

Pretax and interest return on total assets

This ratio enables a reader to determine whether:

(a) The margin on sales earned is reasonable.
(b) Assets of the company are adequately and effectively used.

This is a purer measure of profitability in relation to assets than the return on total assets which is calculated on the net income after tax as interest payments differ between companies as does tax. Reliance Industries Limited has with tremendous forethought and planning, inspite of large profit avoided the payment of tax for years.

ITC Ltd's figures were as follows:—

	30th June 1987	30th June 1986
	Rs. lakhs	Rs. lakhs
Profit before tax	1586	830
Interest	2121	1453
Earning before Interest & Tax	3707	2283
Total assets	37816	38007
Return on average assets	9.8%	

The return could be compared with other tobacco companies to measure which is more profitable or gives a better return to its shareholders.

Return on equity

The return on equity (ROE) measures the return on the investment made by shareholders. It enables one to check whether the returns are adequate and equal to, better or inferior to other alternatives available. This is calculated by expressing as a percentage of shareholder's funds net profit after tax.

The return on equity of two very reputed companies in India are —

	Larsen & Toubro		Hindustan Lever	
	30.9.1986	30.9.85	30.12.86	30.12.85
Profit after tax	3067	3003	3907	3256
Shareholders' Funds	28000	25700	16522	14281
Return on equity (Average)	11.42%		25.37%	

The return on equity of these two companies are though very different high—they cannot be really compared as they are in two different industries.

The return on equity shows the maximum return that is available to shareholders on their investment/stake in the company and this should be considered with other alternatives available at the time of investing in companies.

Return on total invested capital

The return on equity would vary between similar companies and is very dependent on the sources of funds i.e. the ratio of shareholders funds to borrowed funds. In boom years the return on equity of a highly leveraged company (a company very dependant on borrowed funds would be high) whereas in lean years it would be the reverse. On the other hand the return of high equity companies are likely to be low.

A truer measure is, therefore, arrived at by calculating the return on the earnings of a company before interest and tax on total invested capital of the company. Invested capital in this case includes shareholders' funds and borrowings (loans that have an interest cost associated with them.)

Let us look at the return on the two companies examined earlier, Larsen & Toubro & Hindustan Lever.

	Larsen & Toubro		Hindustan Lever	
	30.9.1986	30.9.1985	31.12.86	31.12.85
Profit before tax	3142	3433	6507	5556
Interest	3492	3501	360	391
Earning before interest & tax	6634	6934	6867	5947
Shareholders' funds	28000	25700	16522	14281
Loan funds	35497	29345	6288	8147
Total Invested Capital	63497	55045	22810	22428
Return on average Invested capital	11.19%		30.11%	

This ratio indicates the return earned by the two companies on the funds invested in them. The return should be compared with other similar companies in the same industries and with the industry norm to determine how profitable a particular company is.

As the major aim of a commercial enterprise is profit, the profitability ratios are among the more important group of ratios and must always be examined in depth. All the changes in these ratios must be looked into as these indicate the long term results of the company.

9

ASSET MANAGEMENT & EFFICIENCY

It is important to determine whether a company is utilising its assets efficiently as the entire future of the company—its growth, its expansion and even its very existence may depend on it. It should be therefore examined whether the total amount of each type of asset a company has is reasonable, too high or too low in the light of current and forecasted operating needs. Companies need to, to finance higher levels of working capital at times of growth and to purchase fixed assets at times of expansion, modernisation and rejuvenation, borrow monies or obtain capital from elsewhere. If there are more assets than necessary or if the assets are not being utilised effectively and efficiently the interest paid by the company would be higher than otherwise. In times of recession or depression this can even lead to the death of an otherwise sound company as the company may not be able to, when profits are low, service the high borrowings the company has made. Conversely, should there be fewer assets than is necessary, the company's operations would not be as efficient.

Asset management and efficiency ratios enable one to consider how effectively a company manages its assets. These ratios assume that sales volumes are related to assets over time. Ratios can also be used to assess trends and the efficiency with which the management of a company utilizes its assets. This can be compared with that of the industry and with other companies. It should be remembered that a high asset turnover is not necessarily suggestive of a high return on investment. It could indicate that a company is not keeping adequate levels of assets which could affect its performance in the long run. Asset management ratios are useful too in making forecasts of financial statements.

STOCK TURNOVER

The stock turnover ratio shows the number of times stock

has turned over in a year. This can also be shown as the number of days stocks are held by a company to support sales. As a result this is calculated in two ways—

(a) cost of goods sold divided by average stocks show the times inventory is turned over;
(b) average inventory multiplied by 365 days divided by the cost of goods sold measures stocks in terms of days of sale.

A ratio of 12 times as calculated in (a) above would be 30 days in (b) above and indicates that stocks turnover 12 times a year and that stocks equivalent to 30 days are held to support sales.

Indian Rayon's cost of sales in the year to June 30, 1987 was as follows:

	Rs. lakhs
Opening stock	2418.89
Consumption of Raw Materials	6020.49
	8439.38
Closing stock	2302.61
Cost of sales	6136.77

Its average stock was Rs. 2360.75 lakhs.

The company's stock turned over 2.60 times. The company holds stock to support 140 days sales which is quite high. In some industries stock levels are high due to the process time being long. It may also be high because of the difficulty in selling the company's products. The reader must always try to determine the reason why stocks are high.

Hindustan Lever's figures for the year ended December 31, 1986 shows an entirely different picture—the relevant details are—

	Rs. lakhs
Opening stocks	8,704.52
Raw Materials consumed	39,456.32
	48,160.84
Less: Closing stock	7,161.17
Cost of goods sold	40,999.67

The company's stock turnover is 5.17 times. The number of days in terms of stocks held is 70.62 days.

The ratios held by Indian Rayon and Hindustan Lever are entirely different. These are essentially dependant on the industry in which the company operates. One must always query variations in these ratios between one year and another as this would give an indication of future performance. When the turnover decreases, stocks may not be moving. This could lead to obsolescence. This is especially relevant in hi-tech industries such as the electronics and computer industries.

Accounts payable Ratio

The Accounts payable or creditors ratio shows the period of time the company takes to pay its creditors. It gives an indication of how effectively and how capable the company is in the availing of credit. It can also give hints if the company is going through problems of cash flow and the likes.

The ratio is arrived at by dividing creditors by the cost of goods sold and multiplying the product by 365 in order to express the result in days.

The figures relating to DCM Ltd. for the year to June 30, 1987 are as follows:—

	Rupees
Opening stock	52,20,82,104
Purchase etc.	331,11,39,776
	383,32,21,880
Less: Closing stock	71,53,24,821
Cost of goods sold	311,78,97,059
Creditors (average)	86,00,46,135

The accounts payable ratio is 100.7 days. This means that the company takes approximately 100 days to pay its creditors.

Orkay was a company that was reportedly having cash flow problems. Its figures for the year to March, 31, 1987 are detailed below:—

	1987 Rs. lakhs	1986 Rs: lakhs
Opening stock	2038	1341
Raw Materials etc.	11200	14765
Other Purchases	38	301
	13276	16407
Less: closing stock	1559	2036
Cost of goods sold	11717	14371
Creditors	2245	1384

The ratio in 1987 is, on closing creditors 70 days whereas in 1986 it was only 35 days. The figures have doubled. In this case as opposed to average creditors year end creditors have been taken as there has been a very large increase in the creditors at the year end and it was rumoured that the company had cash flow problems.

There may be situations when the ratio decreases ie. the ratio falls from 45 days to 40 days. This could indicate that the company—

● is not being extended the credit that it had previously received or
● it is not availing the credit being given to it
● is no longer facing the cash flow problems that it was facing earlier.

Whatever be the reason—the reason must be ascertained.

Average collection ratio:

The average collection ratio measures the time taken by customers to pay and indicates the credit policy of the company and determines how effective it is. It also gives an idea on the financial situations of customers. At times of boom, when it is a sellers' market, the average collection period would be very low as due to the scarcity of the product and the demand for it, most sales are made for in cash. At other times, when customers are going through a difficult time, payments will be slow and consequently the average collection ratio will go up. The heavy automobile companies such as TELCO have been experiencing difficulties and their ratios have been on the increase as they have been extending longer payment terms to customers in order to sell their products.

The ratio is calculated by dividing the average receiveables by the sales per day.

Indian Rayon's average sales per day for the year to June 30, 1987 was Rs. 54.73 lakhs. Its average debtors were Rs. 2472.42 lakhs. Its average collection ratio was therefore 45 days. Indian Rayon has to extend credit to its dealers.

ITC Ltd. on the other hand is in an industry which is basically cash oriented. Its daily sales in the year to June 30, 1987 amounted to Rs. 288 lakhs. Its debtors (average) at the year end inclusive of bills discounted, amounted to only Rs. 8269 lakhs. The company's collection period amounted to 29 days. If one calculated this taking into account the deposits it keeps from dealers, this would reduce to a mere 18 days.

This ratio helps management to take timely action to control and effectively manage credit and more importantly cash flow. An increasing ratio can indicate that company is experiencing difficulties in collecting debts and could be considered an early warning sign for large bad debts.

Total asset utilisation

The total asset utilisation ratio is calculated to examine whether a company is generating a sufficient volume of business taking into consideration the size of its asset investment. This ratio is calculated by dividing sales by the average total assets.

The ratio measures the utilisation of the assets of the company and can indicate how effective asset management and capacity utilisation is. It shows how well total assets are generating a certain volume of sales and is a ratio useful in the preparation of forecasts.

The average total assets of Larsen and Toubro Ltd. in the year to 30th September 1986 was Rs. 107977 lakhs. The sales were Rs. 75211 lakhs. The utilisation therefore was 0.69. This should be compared with that of previous years.

Asset management ratios reflect the efficiency of the management and their ability to manage the assets of the company. It indicates the effectiveness of the company's credit policies, the demand for its products and can to an extent reflect whether it is having difficulty in meeting its obligations. The asset management ratios are, therefore, very important in understanding a company.

It must be remembered a deterioration in ratios is not bad. The payable ratio may decrease as a company is paying earlier to take a cash discount. In order to increase sales, it may be extending longer credit terms. Stocks may have increased as the company is expanding its facilities. Hence asset management ratios give pointers to the areas one should examine prior to determining the efficiency of a company.

10

THE AMBIGUITY OF REVENUE RECOGNITION

When does a sale take place? When is the income earned? Revenue recognition is the point in time when the income earned on a sale is accounted for. This in effect should be straight forward. However, as a sale has never been clearly defined in accountancy and as there is no authoritative statement on what constitutes a sale, companies have been known to recognise a sale at situations convenient to them in order to present to shareholders and the public a state of affairs far better than it actually is. A 'real' sale may never have occurred but income would have been recognised and tax and dividends and bonus paid. This has a snowballing effect and can, should times change, result in the company winding up. It is important therefore that while assessing and evaluating a company one should examine the method of revenue recognition.

In the late 1960s there was in the United States of America a tremendous dearth of housing. The government was financing large housing schemes. At this very opportune time, the Stirling family who were well established in construction floated a company called Stirling Homex Ltd. They began initially in manufacturing modular town houses for private developers and later when their modular houses were approved by the government, they began to supply in a large way to government aided housing projects.

Stirling Homex was a well managed company. Its managers were competent and knowledgeable. Its product was very acceptable. In a short while the company became the largest producer of modular homes in the United States. In its very first year its sales was $10.4 millions and its profits were $1.1 million. Within three years, in 1971 its sales grew to $22.5 million. In that year the company, to meet increasing demand, increased its manufacturing facilities and had intentions of floating subsidiaries in other countries to tap into the international markets. It was even contemplating the purchase of ships to transport modular homes to Europe. To finance these the company had a $19 million public issue which was over subscribed. The shares were quoted at a premium and it was considered a "true blue"—the bluest of blue chips. Next Year, in 1972, the COMPANY FILED FOR BANKRUPTCY AND WAS WOUND UP.

What happened? Wall street and the investing public clamoured for reasons. A full investigation was done and it was found that Stirling Homex was recognising profits and income before they were actually earned. This fact was not concealed from the shareholders. It had been mentioned as a note on the accounts. It was simply that nobody had really paid attention to it. The notes to the financial statements for 1971 had a statement that reads "The Company enters into various modular housing sales contracts which contain an allocation of the sales price between modules (based upon published price lists) and installation work. Sales of modules (manufacturing division) are recognised when units are manufactured and assigned to specific contracts. Installation work (installation division) is recorded on the percentage of completion method. The contracts generally provide for payment after receipt of all approvals necessary for occupancy or for payment upon completion of each respective phase. Unbilled receivables represent recorded sales on contracts in process for which billings will be rendered in future in accordance with the contracts."

The note is confusing especially to the layman who would have, after glancing at it, set it aside without actually attempting to determine what it actually means. What does it actually mean? What was the company doing? Briefly the condition of sale was that payment would be made after all approvals. Stirling Homex had expended its manufacturing capacity by 100% and was assuming a sale had taken place as soon as a unit had been manufactured by treating manufacturing as a separate profit centre with utter disregard to when the units would be installed. In 1970 its unbilled dues from clients were $4.6 million. This grew in 1971 to $24.7 million on a sale of only $46.8 million. The company was accounting for profits prior to the installation and acceptance by the customer of the units.

Nearer home, a well known company in the textile industry had a more ingenious method. It had within the main factory several machines for different processes. The chairman formed companies which were owned by his family members or himself and the sole asset of these companies was a machine each. Each time some material went to one of these machines it was assumed a sale took place and bills of exchange were drawn up which were then discounted by banks. The company by this method sold the same item through different companies atleast four times and then discounted the bills of exchange. The monies thus procured were used for various purposes. Monies were thus raised on fictitious sales. "You can't fool everyone all the time." This was found out and the price of the company's shares and its reputation took a nose dive. It also faced a near bankruptcy.

Most companies assume a sale has taken place when the goods leave its premises. This is normally correct as the property passes to the purchaser. However, in some circumstances, companies send goods to dealers with the understanding that should the goods not be sold it would take it back. No monies need be paid till the goods are sold. In this case clearly a sale to a third party had not taken place. However, companies have been known to take items similarly transferred as a sale to boost sales and increase profits. This practice is known as "dealer dumping".

An example of a company that did dealer dumping is JI Case (a U.S. Company). Its notes included the statement "wholesale receivables represent sales to dealers and are paid no later than the dealer sells the equipment." This is prebilling and if the items are not sold but returned the company would be in an awkward position especially as the profits on these items have been accounted for.

Many companies prebill to boost profits. The financial statements for TRW Inc. states "Accounts receivable at December

31, 1982 and 1981 included $307 million and $267 million respectively, relating to longterm contracts and programs of which $141 million and $117 million respectively were unbilled. Unbilled costs, fees and claims represent revenue earned but not billable under terms of the related contracts. Substantially all of such amounts will be billed during the following year as units are delivered and accepted by the customers. Unbilled receivables subject to negotiation were approximately $34 million and $8 million at December 31, 1982 and December 31, 1981 respectively." In this case the company began to take to profits earnings that were yet to be made. Profits were also taken on items that had not been billed and which were under negotiation. This had quadrupled in a year suggesting that the company had the intention of boosting profits as much as possible.

Under normal accounting for insurance the premium relating to a year is taken as that year's income. An insurance company to show great growth took to income in a year all the premiums relating to a policy during its entire life with total disregard to the fact that it related to future years. Once a company does this it has to continue doing so and to show growth it has to sell more and more policies every year. The accounting plot thickens. After a time it cannot keep up and then income as shown in the Profit and Loss begins to decrease. This is what happened to this insurance company. The time came when it could no longer keep up. Sales fell and profits became losses.

In the early eighties Nucorp was the darling of Wall Street. In the first nine months of 1981 profits at $15.6 million was five times the earnings of the complete year 1979. An audit revealed that the company was inflating sales and profits by recognising or accounting for a sale before it actually happens. In this case this began as a part of a conscious decision when it was felt that prebilling and thus accounting for a sale would be the answer for ending the year with a good increase in sales and income. The salesmen had no particular grouse against this as they were paid on sales. The problem arose as the company to show better and yet better results carried on prebilling. At one time prebillings accounted for 60% of the total sales. The company went bankrupt in 1982. It is because of this need to show that one is doing well that one starts prebilling and once started it is difficult to stop.

There was a life assurance company called Equity Funding. It hit upon a really novel idea. It sold to a finance company its rights for future premiums at a discount and then accounted for these as sales in the year. Once started the company had to sell more and more rights to future premiums. The company eventually had no more to sell. It then began to sell rights of fictitious policies. This continued till finally the balloon burst. The company filed for bankruptcy and criminal proceedings were instituted against the senior officers.

J Walter Thompson, one of the largest advertising companies in the world had a subsidiary. Its main purpose was to get local television stations to advertise in net work television. As opposed to being paid the customary 10% the subsidiary was to receive time slots on local television which it would, in turn, sell to its customers at a profit. Revenue was recognised when the time slots were given and not when it was utilised by a client. When a customer did not take a time slot, the slot lapsed. However, this was not reversed as the subsidiary believed that other time slots would be given for those that had lapsed. This practice continued for over two and a half years and it was found out finally that 95 per cent of the sales (income) and the resulting profit were not real.

A hotel was going through hard times. Occupancy had fallen. In order to boost its income it began to recognise income as soon as a booking was made as opposed to doing so only after the customer had stayed at the hotel.

The principle relating to the method of how revenue is recognised is sometimes very ambiguous and this is done on purpose as it gives the company room to manouvre. In Allis Chalmers' 1981 financial statements it is stated "revenue and costs of long term contracts are recognised on the percentage of completion method measured by work performed. Provisions are recorded for losses on contracts whenever it is evident that estimated costs will exceed selling prices." In this the measure of work performed is subjective and on this principle profits can be manipulated.

The above examples show how ingenious managements have taken advantage of a lack of a proper guideline on revenue recognition and applied principles whereby they could project their management in a far better light. This has finally, in most cases, led to the dissolution of the companies as the fictitious sales become larger and more dominant.

What then should be the criterion for recognising sales or revenue? When does it occur? The criteria should be—

(i) all or most of the services to be provided/work to be completed has been done;

(ii) cash or cash equivalents have been received.

(iii) from an economic point of view, revenue should not be recognised until the last major activity is completed and risk and ownership has been passed on to the buyer.

If the above are followed in revenue recognition sales and profits are unlikely to be inflated.

11

THE VALUATION OF STOCKS

Stocks or inventories as they are often termed is the product/products the company makes and sells and earns income on. As a consequence it is probably the most important current asset a company holds. They consist of:

(a) *Raw materials:* the primary purchase which is utilised to manufacture the product/products the company makes.

(b) *Work in progress:* goods that are in the process of manufacture but are yet to be complete.

(c) *Finished goods:* the product/products manufactured by the company that are ready for sale but are yet to be sold.

Stocks are valued at the lower of cost or market value or net realisable value. This is to ensure that there will be no loss at the time of sale as that would have been accounted for. There are many methods of arriving at the value of stocks, the most accepted and common are:

(i) *FIFO or first in first out:* It is assumed, under this method that stocks that come in first would be sold first and those that come in last would be sold last.

Illustration:

On January 1, 1990, Niyva Ltd. purchased 30 televisions at Rs. 8000 each. On March 15, 1990, another 40 televisions were purchased at Rs. 8500 each and on June 1, 1990 a further 20 televisions were purchased at Rs. 9000 each. On June 30, 1990 there were 40 televisions unsold. The value of stocks would be

20 televisions at Rs. 9000 each	1,80,000/-
20 televisions at Rs. 8500 each	1,70,000/-
	3,50,000

(ii) *LIFO or Last in first out:* The premise on which this

method is based is the opposite to that of FIFO. It is assumed that the stocks that arrive last will be sold first. The reasoning is that customers prefer newer materials or products.

Illustration:

If the example of Nivya Ltd. mentioned above is used the value of the 40 televisions unsold on June 30, 1990 would be

30 televisions at Rs. 8000/- each	2,40,000/-
10 televisions @Rs. 8500/- each	85,000/-
	3,25,000/-

The difference may not in one year appear very high but after many years at a time of rising prices, the figures on the Balance Sheet would not be truly reflective of realisable or market value if LIFO is used. This is why FIFO is the more popular method.

Executive and senior management are under enormous pressure to produce greater and yet greater profits and are not beyond tailoring accounting principles and interpreting them to show the results that they wish to show. It is therefore of paramount importance that the reader of an annual report ascertains the manner in which stocks or inventories are valued.

The effect of valuing goods on the LIFO method is best illustrated by the following statement. SCM Corporation's notes to financial statements for the year to June 30, 1978 reads "as of June 30, 1978 approximately 17 per cent of SCM's total inventories were priced on the LIFO method. Had all inventories currently on LIFO been priced on a FIFO basis inventories would have been approximately $18,500,000 higher at June 30, 1978 and $17,600,000 higher at June 30, 1977." Not an inconsiderable amount.

Similarly in the statements of White Consolidated Industries Ltd., it was stated "certain industries are valued on the last in first out method. These inventories which approximated $56,700,000 at December 31, 1975 would have been approximately $24,700,000 higher if they had been valued on a first in first out basis".

When goods are valued on LIFO, the value shown on the Balance Sheet is low (much lower than market value). If more items are sold than were purchased/manufactured the company will have windfall profits.

It is stated in Allis Chalmers' 1981 accounts "1981 and 1980 inventory reductions resulted in liquidation of LIFO inventory quantities carried at costs prevailing in prior years which are one lower than current costs. The effect was to increase 1981 and 1980 net income by $1.3 millions ($4 per share) and $2.7 million ($21 per share) respectively."

The first thing that a reader of financial statements should peruse is the manner in which stocks are valued.

The accounting policies of Hindustan Lever Limited states "Inventories are valued at the lower of cost or estimated net realisable value, after providing for cost or obsolescence. Cost is arrived at mainly on a first in first out basis for every month and where appropriate, includes a proportion of direct production overheads, distribution cost and excise duty."

The manner stocks are valued in Modi Rubber Limited is materially different. In this company, it is stated as follows:-

(a) *Raw materials:* Periodic LIFO except in transit/bonded warehouse and with processors at cost.
(b) *Finished goods:* Lower of cost or realisable value except at overseas depots valued at estimated realisable value. Cost for the purpose of manufactured goods include only direct cost.
(c) *Goods-in-process:* At direct cost."

The auditors' report should be checked as should the accounts for any change in the method of valuation of stock.

In the auditors' report for 1987 of Reliance Industries Ltd. it is stated that there has been a change in the method of valuation of stocks. This is detailed in the notes which reads "Until last year inventories were valued at cost. During the current year the company has changed the method of valuation of inventories and accordingly these are valued at cost or market value whichever is lower. Had the same method been continued inventories and profit would have been higher by Rs. 5.10 crores." This suggests that stocks are being sold at below cost which is of concern. The questions that immediately spring to mind are of the quality of the stocks and the likelihood of their not being sold.

J K Synthetics Ltd. made a loss of Rs. 242.91 lakhs in the year to March 31, 1987. In its notes it is stated "with a view to bring uniformity in the basis of valuation of stocks the method of valuation of finished goods has been modified in respect of two divisions resulting in increase in value of closing stocks by Rs. 24.42 lakhs and decrease in the loss for the year by a similar amount."

A reader of the annual report must always check whether there has been a change in the method of valuation of raw materials, stores and spares, process stocks and finished goods from the method of valuation as previously followed. DCM Ltd.'s annual report for 1986-87 explains the reasons for changes in the method of valuation. The company claims "This is essentially in order to eliminate diversity of practices adopted by the units in this matter and to have uniformity in the method of valuation of all the assets. However at some of the units some further refinement in the valuation is yet to be carried out.

The basis of valuation is now as follows:-

— Raw materials ⎫
— Stores and spares ⎭ at weighted average rates

— Process stocks   At materials cost and direct expenses.

— Finished goods   At materials cost, direct expenses and related overheads.

Consequent to this change the value of closing stocks is higher by Rs. 31.40 lakhs." In this year the company's profit after taxes was Rs. 49.38 lakhs. If Rs. 31.40 lakhs is reduced from this, the profit becomes a mere Rs. 17.98 lakhs.

By inflating or adding to the cost of stocks companies can easily increase the profits. Similarly International Instrument Ltd.'s auditor's report states "In our opinion the valuation of stock is fair and proper and is on the same basis as in the earlier year and is in accordance with the normally accepted accounting principles except in the case of valuation of finished products wherein a certain percentage of administrative overheads including interest charges have been included as was done in the earlier year."

The company has by adding overheads and interest charges which are not clearly identifiable with the cost of production, inflated stocks and therefore profits.

In some industries the risk of obsolescence is very high. This is specially true in the electronics and computer industries where items become inadequate very fast because of newer technology and newer ideas have replaced them. Normal accounting practice requires these to be written down or provided for as they are likely to have to be sold at less than cost. International Instruments Ltd.'s results for the year to September 30, 1987 had the following analysis in its directors' report—

	1986-87 (18 Months) Rs.	1985-86 (12 Months) Rs.
Total Income	82,390,546	111,179,299
Profit before taxation	—	5,022,794
Loss for the period	57,374,735	—
Provision for obsolete/non moving/slow moving/stocks	9,000,000	31,504
Provision for bad and doubtful debts	4,600,000	1,465,145
Profit (Loss) for the period	(70,974,735)	3,526,145

The above suggests that the company has slow moving/obsolete stocks. The question that one should seek answers to are—

(i) Is the provision adequate
(ii) Are there likely to be more items that might become slowmoving/obsolete and if so what is the reason for this.

The answers to these are fundamental for an opinion to be made on the state of affairs on International Instruments Ltd.

111

Sometimes nay often managements do not make provisions as it would affect adversely the results for the year. In Punjab Anand Batteries Ltd.'s notes to the accounts for 1986 it is stated "no provision has been made for nonmoving/slow-moving items of raw materials/components amounting to Rs. 9.5 lakhs, which according to management could be disposed off/used over a period of time. Except for the above, as explained to us, there were no other unserviceable damaged stores and raw materials requiring provision in the opinion of the management." The company did badly in the year making a loss of over Rs. 2 crores. The management wanted it kept at that level and not increased by a further Rs. 9 lakhs.

It is important to determine when stocks actually get sold and ownership passes. Managements have been known to move goods to dealers (dumping on dealers) to recognise revenue and account for profits. One must be careful while reading the statements to ensure that does not happen. In JI Case's accounts it was stated "Wholesale receivables represent sales to dealers and are paid no later than the time the dealer sells the equipment." In short the dealer does not need to pay anything until the goods are sold which means that the rights of ownership have not passed. JI Case took profits for sales that had not actually taken place as a consequence of which sales were overstated and stocks were understated.

In the accounts of Modi Rubber Limited for 1986-87 it was stated "In view of section 438 of the Income-tax Act 1961, during this year, the custom duty, purchase tax/cess on raw materials and stores and spares and excise duty paid on finished goods lying outside factory/goods despatched pending retirement of documents have not been carried in inventories/stocks and correspondingly into direct cost. This has resulted in decrease in the value of stocks of raw materials, stores and spares, finished goods and goods in process by Rs. 157.42 lakhs, Rs. 90.48 lakhs, Rs. 618.81 lakhs and Rs. 6.57 lakhs respectively."

This does explain the manner in which stocks have been valued. This statement suggests that in regard to goods sold, they are not considered actually sold until the documents sent are retired. This is the ultimate precaution.

Stocks as it was mentioned earlier is an immensely important asset and because of its nature and the many ways it can be manipulated the reader of an annual report or an analyst must necessarily examine the method of valuation of stocks and read the notes to the accounts extremely carefully.

12

FIXED ASSETS & DEPRECIATION

Fixed assets are assets owned by a company that have a useful life of many years and are utilised by the company in the daily course of its business. The most common fixed assets a company has are land, buildings, plant, machinery, furniture, fittings, equipment and motor vehicles.

All the assets mentioned above except land have a useful life—the period ofcourse varies from asset to asset and because of this their value diminishes as time goes on. A two year old car cannot be considered to be of equal value to a brand new one. This is because its useful life has reduced and there has been wear and tear. The writing off of an asset over its useful life is known as depreciation. The purpose of depreciation too is to have at the end of the useful life of an asset an amount set aside as a provision which would be equal to the original cost of the asset.

Fixed assets are shown on the Balance Sheet of a company at cost or revaluation less accumulated depreciation. Companies are required to detail in the schedules to the Balance Sheet the movement of the fixed assets during the year. A typical movement schedule of fixed assets is exhibited Exhibit 'I' (pg. 122).

It is also a requirement that a company states the manner in which it values its assets and calculates depreciation. ITC Limited states its policy on fixed assets as follows:—

I.T.C. LIMITED

"Significant Acccounting policies

It is Corporate Policy.

FIXED ASSETS

To state Fixed Assets at cost of acquisition inclusive of inward freight duties and taxes and incidental expenses related to acquisition. In respect of major projects involving construction—related pre-operational expenses form part of the value of the assets capitalised.

To adjust the original costs of Fixed Assets acquired through Foreign Currency Loans at the end of each financial year by any change in liability arising out of expressing the outstanding foreign loan at the rate of exchange prevailing at the date of the Balance Sheet.

DEPRECIATION

To calculate depreciation on Fixed Assets in a manner that amortises the cost of the assets after commissioning, over their estimated useful lives by equal annual instalments. No depreciation is charged in the year of disposal.

REVALUATION OF ASSETS

To review the original book value of assets, from time to time, and revalue such of those assets as have appreciated in value significantly, in order to relate them more closely to current replacement values, to adjust the provision for depreciation on such revalued assets, where applicable, in order to make allowance for consequent additional diminution in value on considerations of age, condition and unexpired useful life of such assets; to transfer to Revaluation Reserve the difference between the written up value of the assets revalued and depreciation adjustment and to charge Revaluation Reserve Account with annual depreciation on that portion of the value which is written up."

The reader of an annual report must be aware of the following:—

Revaluation

Usually fixed assets are stated on the Balance Sheet at historical cost i.e. at the price originally paid for it. Often this is much lower than the current market value—especially if the asset (example land) had been purchased forty or fifty years earlier. By not disclosing the actual current value the company is understating its shareholders' funds and has hidden reserves. Often, however, to reflect current values and also to show that the assets of the company have increased in value, assets are assessed and the market value is stated in the Balance Sheet. The increase between cost and market value is as it is not a realised amount credited to a revaluation reserve. This may not be distributed (the profit arising on revaluation) as it is not a realised profit.

A typical statement on the revaluation of assets is stated in the notes forming part of the accounts of Blue Star Ltd. for 1987.

"Land, Buildings and Plant and Machinery have been revalued at 1-7-1985 by the valuers Messrs S.R. Batliboi Consultants Pvt. Ltd. The net amount written up on revaluation as at 1-7-1985 was as shown below:-

	Rupees
Land freehold)	86,55,137
Land (leasehold)	19,38,644
Building	3,30,06,778
Plant & Machinery	1,81,63,403
Total	6,17,63,962

Provision for depreciation for the year on the above-mentioned net increase due to Revaluation for the year has been calculated as per straight line method over the residual life of such assets indicated by the valuers, resulting in an additional charge of Rs. 18,20,748 (previous year Rs. 18,65,999). An equivalent amount has been transferred to the Profit & Loss Account from Revaluation Reserve."

In ITC's notes to the accounts for the year to June 30, 1987 it is stated "a revaluation of freehold land, freehold buildings and leasehold property carried out by an approved valuer as at 30th June 1986 had resulted in an increase in the gross value of assets over original cost by Rs. 1,17,62 lakhs (freehold land Rs. 49.56 lakhs, freehold buildings Rs. 63.51 lakhs and leasehold properties Rs. 4.55 lakhs) including Rs. 95.41 lakhs increase, which had arisen as a result of a revaluation of the company's freehold land and freehold buildings on 30th June, 1983 after taking into account subsequent withdrawals and Rs. 22.21 lakhs increase arising out of the current revaluation. The accumulated depreciation adopted on the basis of the revaluation of freehold land, freehold buildings and leasehold property on 30th June 1986 and adjusted against the revaluation at current replacement values was Rs. 28.79 lakhs (freehold buildings Rs. 27.93 lakhs and leasehold property Rs. 0.86 lakhs) to date including Rs. 186 lakhs (freehold buildings Rs. 100 lakhs and Leasehold property Rs. 0.86 lakhs) representing the additional amount arising out of the latter revaluation. The net increase in value resulting from the revaluation carried out on 30th June 1986 of Rs. 20.35 was credited to revaluation reserve.

Gross depreciation for the current year is Rs. 826 lakhs of which Rs. 131 lakhs has been transferred to Revaluation reserve."

Normally, as the assets grow older, a portion of the revaluation reserve is written back to profits in such a manner that at the end of the useful life of the asset, the depreciation will be equal to the value of the asset and at that time the revaluation reserve will be nil.

The revaluation reserve of ITC Ltd. in 1987 was as follows:—

	(Rs. in lakhs)	
	1987	1986
At commencement of year	8883	6996
Less: to Profit & Loss Account		
— Depreciation	(131)	(148)
— Sales of Fixed Assets	(12)	—
Add: During the year	—	2035
	8740	8883

Gradually the balance in the Revaluation Reserve will be written back to the Profit and Loss account.

There is a note in the accounts of International Instruments Ltd's fixed assets schedule that "the company has revalued as on March 31, 1986 part of its land and buildings on the basis of valuation by the Registered Architect and a net sum of Rs. 31,479,152 lakhs has been added to the cost of land and building by creating the revaluation reserve by equal amount." The revaluation reserve is a paper profit and not an actual profit and should not be reduced unless there is an adequate depreciation provision. The company had an extremely bad year and the company reduced its entire balance of Rs. 27,75,715 stating "amount shown as deduction from debit balance in Profit and Loss Account." This is not correct as in effect the revaluation reserve which is a paper profit has been used to reduce the debit balance on the profit and loss account which is an actual loss.

Capitalisation of Interest

Companies did for many years capitalise (add to the cost of fixed assets) interest paid to acquire fixed assets.

Illustration

Nivya Ltd. borrowed Rs. 10,00,000 at 14%p.a. to purchase a machine. The loan and interest was paid for at the end of 12 months, the payments being —

Principal	1,000,000
Interest	140,000
	1,140,000

The company would state the cost of the machinery to be Rs. 1,140,000 as the interest expense was incurred purely for the purchase of acquiring the machinery.

The main reason this was done was by this the company could spread the interest cost over the life of the asset as opposed to bearing it in the first year which would have meant a big drop in profits.

The Institute of Chartered Accountants have ruled against this practice as it has an effect of overstating the actual cost.

However, some companies did not do so. A classic example is the Star Industrial and Textile Enterprises Ltd. In its report for the year ended December 31, 1985 it is stated "interest payable on borrowings related to the acquisition of fixed assets has been capitalised for the period during which the assets were in use for commerical production. This is contrary to accounting

practice recommended by the Institute of Chartered Accountants of India and subsequently the loss after charging
depreciation on capitalised interest has been understated by
Rs. 4,21,084.00, the gross block of fixed assets have been
overstated by Rs. 10,03,414.00 and reserves and surplus have
been overstated by Rs. 5,82,330.00 as compared to the position which would have prevailed if the recommended practice
had been followed."

Extra Shift depreciation

If a machine is used in two or more shifts its useful life would be
shorter than if it is used for only one shift. It is therefore normal
and usual for extra shift or multiple shift depreciation to be
calculated. Often companies do not do so since the extra
depreciation is an additional charge on the profits of the
company and most companies are constantly trying to show
higher and higher profits.

The auditors of Orkay Silk Mills Ltd. in the report for 1986-87
stated "the company has provided depreciation at rates which
are determined on a single shift basis without considering the
extra and multiple shift allowances which is contrary to the
accounting practice recommended by the Institute of
Chartered Accountants of India. Had such allowances been
considered the charge for depreciation would have been
higher by Rs. 3,51,43,708." The profit of the company was
Rs. 784 lakhs in that year. If additional depreciation had been
accounted for, the profit would have been only Rs. 433 lakhs
which is lower by 45%.

In Star Textiles' report for 1985, it is similarly stated
"Depreciation in respect of extra shift allowance amounting to
Rs. 17,26,636 relating to plant and machinery has not been
provided. This is contrary to the accounting practice re-
commended by the Institute of Chartered Accountants of
India. Consequently Loss for the year is lower by
Rs. 17,26,636/- and reserves and surplus as well as net block of
fixed assets are higher by Rs. 97,71,356 (previous year
Rs. 80,44,720/-) as compared to the position which would have
prevailed if recommended practice had been followed."

Actual existence

The reader of an annual report should also check to see

whether the fixed assets actually exists. This can be seen from the Auditors Report as they are required to certify whether assets have been physically verified during the year and comment on them. In situations where there is doubt, the auditors are expected to state their concern. The Auditors' Report of International Instruments Ltd. included the following statement:—

"The Company is maintaining proper records to show full particulars including quantitative details of land, vehicles and a major portion of plant and machinery and buildings. We are informed by the Management that in respect of Fixed Assets other than those mentioned above the work of compiling full particulars with quantitative details and situation is still under progress. We are informed by the Management that major portion of the fixed assets have been physically verified during the financial year ended 30.09.83 and the differences found on such verifications are said to be still in the process of reconciliation."

It is hoped that the date mentioned above of 30.09.83 is a printing error. If not the time taken to reconcile is unreasonable and of concern. It is to be noted that the records of fixed assets do not agree with the physical verification taken. It is more than likely that some may have to be written off which effectively means an increase in the loss.

The schedule of fixed assets shows that the machinery in transit on 31.3.1986 and 30.09.1987 (a gap of 18 months) was Rs. 324,752 which appears unusual. This must be queried as it is most unusual for machines to be in transit for 18 months.

Change in accounting policy

Whenever there is a change from accounting policies it is necessary for this to be clearly mentioned.

In Blue Star Limited's annual report for 1987 it is stated "The Company has been making provision for depreciation on fixed assets consistently on the written down value method using the rates prescribed by the Income-tax Rules. For the company's accounting year ended June 30, 1987, the prescribed rates of depreciation have been considerably enhanced. The

Board is of the view that provision for depreciation on the basis of such enhanced rates amounting to Rs. 1,61,02,012 would be excessive and would not give a true and fair view of the profit for the year since the useful life of the Fixed Assets is far longer than that envisaged by the revised ncome-Tax Rules. Hence the Board has decided to provide for depreciation to Rs. 98,42,621 consistent with past practice using the rates applicable for the previous year, which they consider reasonable and adequate.

The difference in depreciation amounting to Rs. 62,59,391 has been appropriated to Capital Reserve. The Board considers this amount as not free for dividend for the year ended June 30, 1987".

In effect the Company has changed its accounting policies and had it been consistent with previous practice the profits would have been lower by Rs. 62.59 lakhs. Let us now examine the effect it would have had on the profits for the year.

	(Rs. in lakhs)	
	1987	1986
Profit before taxation	364.55	311.53
Additional depreciation	62.59	—
	301.96	311.53
Provision for taxation	110.00	90.00
Profit after taxation	191.96	221.53

It would be observed that the profit has fallen by 13.3 per cent had depreciation been calculated on a consistent basis.

The reader of an annual report would be wise to examine fixed assets and depreciation.

EXHIBIT 'I'

LIPTON INDIA LIMITED

(Rupees in lakhs)

4 Fixed Assets	Cost as at 30th June, 1986	Additions	Disposals and Adjustments	Cost as at 30th June, 1987	Depreciation as at 30th June, 1987	Net Book Value as at 30th June, 1987	Net Book Value as at 30th June, 1986
Land—Freehold	16.99	—	—	16.99	—	16.99	16.99
Leasehold	2.57	—	—	2.57	—	2.57	2.57
Buildings	220.55	13.92	—	234.47	89.71	144.76	143.54
Plant and Machinery	840.34	169.07	5.36	1,004.05	547.78	456.27	404.69
Railway Sidings	1.96	—	—	1.96	0.77	1.19	1.39
Vehicles	26.17	0.87	1.11	25.93	17.45	8.48	9.71
Furniture, Fittings etc.	111.77	35.83	1.07	146.53	70.03	76.50	61.66
	1,220.35	219.69	7.54	1,432.50	725.74	706.76	640.55
Previous Year	1,036.30	202.65	18.60	1,220.35	579.80	640.55	

Title Deeds of immovable properties acquired from Hindustan Lever Limited, are still in the process of being transferred in the name of the Company. Buildings include those on leasehold land.

13

INTANGIBLE ASSETS

There are assets which provide benefits to a company but do not have any physical form. Such assets are known as intangible assets. These assets are in real effect expenditure incurred by a company that are yet to be written off. They are often not written off in the year the expense is incurred on the argument that the benefit that accrues as a consequence extends over many years. They are therefore expensed off over the period the benefit that arises due to the expenditure extends to the company. The usual intangible assets that one comes across on the Balance Sheet of companies are — research costs, advertising costs, patents, trade secrets, knowhow, preliminary expenses, share issue expenses and the likes.

The major problem that arises with intangible assets is to determine whether the expenditures have future benefits and can be quantified with some degree of accuracy so they can be capitalised and amortised (written off over a period of time) or whether they have no future benefits and are therefore expenses of the period in which they are incurred. Another problem is to determine the period the benefit is to extend (2 years or 5 years or whatever) and the method of amortisation that should be used to write this off.

At this juncture it is important to examine the more common intangible assets.

Research and development: Many companies especially the pharmaceutical companies incur large expenditure on research and development. This is to develop a technological or marketing advantage and to be more competitive or to improve upon an old product. Whatever be the reason, research costs do yield benefits in the future. The question therefore arises—should they be charged to expenses immediately or capitalised and amortised over a period of time.

Companies used diverse methods till finally an accounting standard was issued. Under generally accepted accounting principles (G A A P) research and development costs must be expensed immediately. The reasoning for this is that the future benefits of research and developments costs are too uncertain and it is therefore prudent to write these off. Furthermore, if they are to be capitalised, then in fairness each research project must be analysed to determine whether there is likely to be a future benefit and then the period the benefit is likely to extend must be ascertained. This is difficult, subjective and abstract.

Advertising: The argument extended for capitalising advertising expenses is that the benefits of advertising campaigns usually extends for a period of time after the costs are incurred. Normal practice is to expense all advertising expenses as it is impossible to determine the period the benefits of advertisements and advertising campaigns are likely to extend to and the expenses incurred year after year are roughly similar.

Patent is a right obtained to exclude others from profiteering on an invention made. If the patent is purchased its cost is normally capitalised and this is written off over the life of the patent. If it is developed inhouse the cost is usually written off under research and development costs.

Share issue/debenture issue expenses: The costs relating to a share issue or debenture issue are large. There are costs connected with advertising, underwriting, fees to issue managers, processing costs and a host of other expenses. The writing off these in a single year, it is argued, will distort the profit and loss account and it is also argued that as the benefits of the capital raised through the issue will be for some considerable period of time that the expense should be written off over a period of time.

Goodwill: This is an intangible asset and is the difference between the purchase price of a unit and the value of its net assets. Most companies in India show this as a fixed asset and this is usually not depreciated.

Let us now examine the intangible asset as seen in the published figures of Indian companies.

In the 20th Annual Report and Accounts 1985-86 of Gangappa Industries Ltd. the miscellaneous expenditure not written off was as follows:

	1986	1985
Capital issue Expenses	3,06,850	3,06,850
Expenditure on New Projects	89,126	89,126
Deferred Revenue Expenditure	1,17,000	1,17,000
Research and Development expenditure	1,91,405	1,91,405
	7,04,381	7,04,381

It would be immediately noted that there has been no movement in the year. The company had made a loss before tax and adjustments of Rs. 68,21,776 and did not want to increase this by a further amount. The Institute of Chartered Accountants have very clearly stated that certain expenses such as research and development expenditure, advertising expenditure and other revenue expenditure should be writtenoff in the year the expense is incurred as it is clearly not possible to actually quantify or state the period the benefit arising from the expenditure will extend. It is even arguable whether any benefit at all will extend from the expense incurred.

Similarly the Annual Report of Punjab Anand Batteries Limited for 1985-86 had in its Balance Sheet miscellaneous expenditure which was made up of:

	1986	1985
Deferred revenue expenditure, Share/Debenture/Right Share	Rs. 5,08,001	Rs. 5,80,572
Issue expenses	Rs. 11,13,831	Rs. 12,07,345
Preliminary expenses	—	Rs. 7,247
Development expenditure pending allocation	—	Rs. 9,77,911
	Rs. 16,21,832	Rs. 27,73,075

In this case the company has consciously been charging to profits a portion of the miscellaneous expenditure. However, when assessing the company the reader must remember that Rs. 16 lakhs worth of assets have no tangible value and must be reduced from total assets.

In the 1985 Annual report of Star Industrial and Textile Industries Limited the miscellaneous expenditure carried forward in the Balance Sheet is as follows:

	Rupees 1985	Rupees 1984
Debenture issue expenses	21,40,593	42,81,186
Deferred export promotional expenses	64,32,649	75,18,959
	85,73,242	1,18,00,145

The company had obviously spent an enormous amount on export promotional trips. It was probably more than the company could bear and if it had been expensed in the year the expense was incurred it would have brought the company to its knees. It was therefore deferred to be written off over five years.

It is stated in the auditors report of International Instruments Ltd. for 1987 that "amount due and payable to employees who have opted for retirement under early/voluntary retirement schemes treated as deferred revenue expenditure— Rs. 175.77 lakhs." An examination at this time of the breakup of the miscellaneous expenditure account yet to be written off shows the following:

		Rupees
(a)	expenses in connection with issue of shares and debentures	530,957
(b)	Project expenses	3,112,467
(c)	early retirement benefits	17,576,569
(d)	Technical knowhow fees	2,631,700
		23,851,693

The expenses detailed above are not assets at all. Project expenses should have been written off as should have been early retirement benefits. Technical knowhow fees too should be written off as it does not have any tangible existence.

Another item that does not have any tangible existence but is carried forward year after year and more often than not—with no amortisation or reduction is goodwill. Goodwill is the value of the name and prestige a company has acquired over a period of time. It is difficult to calculate goodwill and in company accounts goodwill really represents the difference between the purchase price of a company acquired and the market value of its net assets. Many companies do show goodwill in their accounts.

1. In Blowplast Ltd. it is   Rs. 84,000
2. In ITC Ltd. it is   Rs. 490,000
3. In Orkay Silk Mills Ltd. it is   Rs. 280,000

Goodwill is shown in the accounts of many American companies too.

The notes to the financial statements of White Consolidated Industries Inc. reads "the excess of cost over purchased net assets is being carried at cost and not being amortised because in the opinion of the management, there has not been any decrease in the value of the asset."

A similar statement is made in the financial statements of Colt Industries Inc. and subsidiaries "excess costs arising from acquisitions prior to October 31, 1970 ($10,466,000) are not amortised or written off unless there is a dimunition in value of the acquired company." This statement is made because it was made mandatory that after 1971 in USA that all goodwill be amortised and written off.

TRW Inc's Annual Report probably best explains it. "Intangibles arising from acquisitions consummated prior to 1971 (approximately $104 million) are not being amortised, because, in the opinion of the management there is no present indication of diminished value. Intangibles arising from acquisition in 1971 and thereafter are being amortised as required by generally accepted accounting principles by the straight line method over a period not to exceed 40 years." It would be agreed that if the goodwill of $104 million is written off the net income of the company would be seriously hurt.

Stirling Homex's 1971 Accounts showed the following deferred assets:

	Amortisation period	1971 (in dollars)	1970
Patents pending/ trademarks	Legal Life	1,71,680	88,660
Training & professional development	3 years	4.91,641	1,48,636
Research and development	5 years	6,71,897	84,496
Project and production start up costs	2 to 5 years	8,44,028	5,03,539
Property acquisition costs		3,79,546	1,18,778
		25,58,792	9,44,109

The company did not write many of these expenses off as it wished to, at this time, show large and impressive profits.

Although the managements of companies argue that the reason why intangible assets such as advertising costs, research and developments costs etc. are not written off immediately is because the benefits that accrue to the company would stretch for a long period of time, the reader of a report would be wise to remember that the intangible asset has no real value especially if it is a deferred expense. He should therefore not take this into consideration when evaluating the company.

14

CONTINGENT AND OTHER LIABILITIES

A contingent liability may be defined as a liability that might crystallise on the happening of an event. Whether the event would occur or not is uncertain and is usually dependent on something else. On the assumption that it may not take place and the liability would not crystallise no provisions are usually made in the books of accounts apart from a note in the accounts so that shareholders and readers of the financial statements are aware of the risks.

Normally most of the contingent liabilities remain contingent liabilities and rarely crystallise into real or actual liabilities but they can and this is why one should be aware of them and one should consider them when evaluating or forming an opinion on the strengths and viability of a company.

What are the kind of contingent liabilities one comes across and what are its implications?

1. Damages

D.C.M. Limited's Annual Report for 1986-87 had in its notes to the accounts the following "in respect of the accidental oleum gas leak which occurred in the previous year in one of the units of the company, the Supreme Court in its judgement of 20th December, 1986 by an order directed that the claims will be scrutinised and processed by the Delhi Legal Aid and Advisory Board and subsequently disposed off in the appropriate Court.............. In view of the uncertainty of the legal position prevailing in respect of the matter, there is as yet no clear basis for the company to make an estimate of the quantum of liability which may eventually devolve on the company. However, the company has an insurance cover of Rs. 2 crores against the accident." This statement informs the reader of a liability that might have to be paid. The company is insured for this upto Rs. 2 crores but if it exceeds that the company would be out of funds.

2. Excise Claims

The reports of many companies contain notes regarding excise claims which are disputed by the company. These are sometimes partly provided for. In most cases the amounts are not very material.

However, in some cases they could be and threaten even the very existence of the company. The note to schedule 17 of the accounts of ITC Ltd. for the year to June 30th 1987 had a statement. "The Supreme Court passed an order in May 1983 on the interpretation of section 4 of the Central Excise & Salt Act 1944 and subsequently passed final judgement in this regard. The appeals related to ITC Ltd. have not yet been disposed off by the Supreme Court. The Directors are of the opinion that the company's liability, after taking into account the mutual claims of both parties, has been fully ascertained and taking into consideration the provisions made in previous years and the charge to the Profit & Loss Account in these accounts, the liability has been finally dealt with. However final order relating to this matter is yet to be passed by the Supreme Court."

This would tend to make a shareholder feel comfortable but this is not so as the Directors' Report has a statement, "Consequent upon a search and seizure conducted by the Excise authorities, a show cause Notice dated 27th March 1987 was issued to your company for alleged evasion of excise duty during the period 1st March, 1983 to 28th February 1987. The charge is based on the premise that your company allegedly colluded with retailers in selling cigarettes at a price higher than that printed on the package, which was the basis of levying duty during the aforesaid period. Your Company has therefore been asked to show cause as to why it should not be required to pay duty at the higher slab corresponding to the actual price allegedly charged by the retailers, amounting to an unprecedented sum of Rs. 803.78 crores besides other penalties in law. The Calcutta High Court has admitted a petition on 14th August 1987 filed by your Company, challenging the validity of the Show Cause Notice." It goes on to say "the Collector of

Central Excise, Patna by two Show Cause Notices dated 3rd July, 1987 has reopened some issues in respect of despatches from your company's factory at Monghyr. The duty allegedly evaded and now claimed has been estimated at Rs. 43.48 crores, besides penalties as provided in law. Your attention is drawn to the Note in schedule 17 of the Accounts (detailed above) and it is reiterated that in the opinion of your Directors, your company has no further liability in respect of these matters."

It is noted that the company lost the petition challenging the validity of the Show cause notice in December 1987. The possibility of the company losing the case exists. The total claim amounts to Rs. 847.26 crores. The networth of the company at that time was only Rs. 166.48 crores. If the claim or even a portion of it is held payable the company would be bankrupt. Albeit this may take time but the possibility exists and the reader must be aware and remember this at the time of evaluating the company.

3. Gratuity

Many companies account for gratuity on a cash basis and do not provide for the full amount payable on the date of the Balance Sheet. This is on the argument that the company is a going concern and that it is unlikely that the company would need to pay the full amount of the gratuity liability.

The manner in which this is mentioned in the statements vary and some examples are as follows:

(a) In DCM Ltd's notes it is stated "Gratuity is accounted for on payment basis. The total liability is estimated at Rs. 2770.00 lakhs (1985-86 = Rs. 2574.46 lakhs) net of tax of Rs. 1315.75 lakhs (1985-86 = Rs. 1287.23 lakhs) against which there is a balance of Rs. 390.12 lakhs (1985-86 = Rs. 390.12 lakhs) in the Reserve Account. This liability is not calculated on an actuarial basis but represents the amount of accrued liability calculated on the basis of eligibility under the payment of gratuity Act/Company's own Gratuity Schemes."

This means that the liability has been calculated on only those who are eligible (who have had more than 5 years service). If it had been done on an actuarial basis, the liability would have been higher.

(b) The liability for Indian Rayon was however arrived at differently. It is stated in its notes "Gratuity liability as per actuarial valuation not provided for, which is accounted for on cash basis Rs. 436.69 lakhs.

In both the cases the company accounts for gratuity only when it pays it. Should the company wind up then the liability would crystallise.

4. Claims not acknowledged as debts

There may be, at the date of the Balance Sheet, claims on the company by third parties, which the company may feel is not justifiable and as a consequence have not provided for them.

In Hindustan Lever's Accounts to December 31, 1986 it is stated "claims made against the company not acknowledged as debts—gross Rs. 17,00.69 lakhs (1985 = Rs. 13,80.21 lakhs).

Although the amount is large, the company would usually have reason for not providing for them and if it is unlikely to crystallise into an actual liability there is no reason why a provision should be made.

5. Uncalled Liability on shares partly paid

Often, when shares are issued by companies, at the time of application only 50% of the issue price needs to be paid—the balance being payable on allotment and/or one or more calls.

On the Balance Sheet date there may be amount due on shares that have been partly paid up—the uncalled liability on these shares have to be shown as a contingent liability as it can be called up at any time.

6. Bills discounted but not matured

Companies in order to improve their cashflow discount bills of exchange with their bankers. This is also sometimes done to windowdress the accounts—to reduce debtors and overdrafts.

If the bills are not paid or if they are dishonoured the company can be called upon to pay the bank the amount of the bill. There is therefore a liability which is contingent upon the bill being dishonoured. In some companies this may be large and therefore this is mentioned in the notes to the accounts.

Many readers of Annual Reports argue that this should be adjusted for in the accounts as this results in an artificial reduction in debtors and bank overdrafts.

7. Guarantees

In many situations companies are required to hand over bank guarantees which become payable should an event occur or if performance of the contract for which the guarantee is required is not done by a stipulated date. At the time the bankers issue the guarantee they normally insist on the company issuing a counter guarantee.

There is a contingent liability in this case that should there be a default the guarantee may be called upon and the bank would have to pay the person/entity to whom the guarantee has been issued. In this situation the bank would call upon the company to pay on the counter guarantee given by the company.

8. Foreign Exchange Liabilities

In recent years many companies have been availing of loans denominated in foreign currencies for the purchase of machinery, raw materials, ships and the likes. As the rates in foreign exchange fluctuate there is always a possibility of the company losing a considerable amount should the other currency strengthen against the rupee. This has happened in a number of instances where Swiss Franc denominated loans have been taken.

In Reliance Industry Ltd.'s notes to the accounts for the year to December 31, 1986 it is stated—

"(a) Foreign Currency loans availed of during the year to acquire plant and machinery have been accounted for in terms of Indian Rupees at the exchange rates prevailing on relevant dates.

(b) No effect has been given in the Accounts to the fluctuations in rates of exchange on outstanding balance of foreign exchange loans."

(c) The Company has consistently been treating difference on account of fluctuations in exchange rates on payments of instalments of loans, deferred credit facilities etc. as a revenue expenditure and the same amounting to Rs. 4.32 crores (previous year Rs. 3.39 crores) has been included under the head "General expenses."

This would explain to the reader that fluctuations in foreign exchange has been amounting to losses of Rs. 4 crores every year. The total likely loss of course is not quantifiable as it is not possible to forecast and provide for the likely fluctuations. Very often to hedge against this likely loss companies book forward contracts in foreign exchange.

The effect of changes is also mentioned in Orkay Silk Mills' Annual Report 1986-87. "Consequent to the realignment of the value of the foreign currency loans, the rupee liability of the company in respect of such loans increased by Rs. 9,14,78,490. As a result, the value of Plant and Machinery has been increased in the books of account as on March 31, 1987 by Rs. 9,14,78,490 (1986 = Rs. 249,96,433)."

9. Tax Liabilities

There may be tax liabilities which have not been provided for. There may be claims on the company by the Income-tax authorities which the company may not have provided for. Or the company may have claimed for allowances as a consequence of which there is no liability. These may not all be allowable and a contingent liability may exist. In Reliance Industry Limited's accounts to December 31, 1986, it is stated "The company has been advised that there will be no tax liability for the year ending December 31, 1986, in view of various reliefs claimed in tax proceedings. The Company is of the opinion that the Taxation Reserve of Rs. 10 crores created in the previous year is adequate to take care of tax liability, if any, for pending assessments." The wording is exceedingly noncommittal and vague and the reader must remember a claim could arise that has not been provided for.

Reliance Industries had also, in its accounts a contingency income-tax liability for Rs. 6.10 crores.

10. Contracts remaining to be executed

At the year end there are often contracts remaining to be executed of a capital nature which have not been provided for. This occurs when a contract has been entered into for the building of a factory and/or the purchase of machinery. The amounts are not accounted for as the contract has not been completed. However a contingent liability exists as when the work is completed the company is bound to pay for it. The contingent liability of Reliance Industries regarding this was Rs. 301.78 crores in 1986.

The other kinds of contingent liabilities that one comes across normally in the Notes to the Financial Statements of companies are—

(a) Bonds executed in favour of Excise and Customs Authorities;
(b) Indemnities toward export obligations against capital goods import.
(c) Guarantees to Banks against credit facilities given to subsidiaries or associate companies.
(d) Export bills discounted against irrevocable letters of credit.

It must be remembered that many of these contingent liabilities may never crystallise into an actual liability but some may and these are the ones that cause concern and they could have a material effect on the financial viability of the entire enterprise. The reader of Annual Reports must weigh and consider the contingent liabilities of a company. He ignores them at his risk.

PART III

15

MANAGEMENT

Upon the quality and the competence of the management of a company rests the prospects say the very existence of a company. A good, innovative management can make a company grow and a bad one can kill it. Chrysler in the United States was an ailing giant. Iacocca, with shrewd policies and tight, tough management made it profitable once more. Nearer home, Burroughs Wellcome declared a loss a year ago on account of its diversification not turning out to be the success hoped for. A year later with a new chief executive at its helm, the company was back with a bang— its most recent financial statements show the company is back on track. Metal Box was a decade ago among the most respected names in India's corporate galaxy. On account of a series of occurrences including diversifications that went wrong, in late 1987/early 1988 the company closed down all its factories—a happening without precedent. The company inducted a man with a reputation of being able to save companies from the very teeth of death. A factory was opened in mid 1988 and began making profits in the very first month. Whether this man Krishna, on whose shoulder the mantle of savior has been placed would be able to actually save Metal Box is yet to be seen. What is evident is the fact of recognition by all that the man at the helm can determine the fortunes of a company and it is for this reason that no one should invest in a company, no one should lend to a company, no one should have a stake in a company without having first assessed its management.

In India, management can be broadly divided into two—

● Family Management
● Professional Management

Family Management

Family managed companies are those where the seats of

power are occupied by members of a family and the mantle of leadership or control of the affairs of such companies are passed from family member to family member; from father to son, from brother to brother and from uncle to nephew.

In these companies the management runs the company very often as its own. The decisions are made with the family interests in view. The employees including the senior manager are considered paid employees of the family and are, unfortunately at times, treated as such. I remember an incident that happened many years ago but which has cast an indelible mark in my mind. It was at Bombay airport. I was going abroad and as I was about to go through to immigration I witnessed the departure of the head of a large business house for a trip abroad. The chief executives of his companies were around him—men famous in their fields— respected and competent. When their leader was about to go through immigration these captains of industry (some much older than their master) bent double and touched their leader's feet as a sign of respect or subservience (I know not which) and their heads were touched as a sign of blessing by their master with a smile of satisfaction. I dread to think what would have happened to the career of one of these captains of industry had he not touched his chairman's feet. In short, employees in family managed companies are expected to be subservient to the family and family loyalty is one of the most important attributes required. Loyalty to the family is rewarded too. If a retainer is ill he is looked after and when he retires he is given a good pension. A loyal executive of a very large family managed company in Calcutta died a premature death. The company gave his wife a job and helped in the education of her children. Very few multinationals would do this.

Family managed companies are usually rigid in its views— orthodox and traditional. This has been mainly on account of family businesses being managed at the helm by patri- archs who had not been exposed to modern methods of management. The sons of the family reared to represent their elders have bowed to their ways. These are changing now. The scions of the large business houses have gone abroad. Many have been educated at the more prestigious business schools and many of them are now managing their businesses. Change has crept in. Modern methods of management are being used effectively and the businesses are thriving. Yet, in spite of it all in family managed businesses, at the end it is the family that matters and it is the family that decides on what course of action should be taken, what should be done and at the helm—the chief executive will always be a family member.

Professional Management

Professionally managed companies are those that are managed by employees, by persons who do not usually have a financial stake in the company and have been chosen to manage the company due to their proven competence and professional qualifications and ability.

Professional managers depend on success in achieving their goals to retaining their positions. They are constantly set targets of growth to achieve. As a consequence they tend to be efficient, cost effective and stable. There is usually a science or a logic in the manner they manage the business and arrive at their decisions and as they are accountable for these to a Board of Directors and ultimately the shareholders they are usually careful and conscientious. Professional managers retain their position by "delivering the goods" and in order to do so and to meet greater and greater demands and higher targets they are prepared to listen to new ideas and try out new products. They are receptive and to ensure that their methods are the best they try to be aware of the latest breakthroughs in science, technology, electronics and management science.

As a consequence professionally managed companies are normally well organised, growth oriented and good performers. Investors are the recipients of regular dividends and bonus issues. This is good.

However, there is, in professionally managed companies, a lot of infighting and internal politics. Managers are, as their promotions etc. entirely dependant on performance, always trying to outshine one another or attempting to destroy a competing manager's credibility. This does not happen usually in family managed concerns as all are aware that at the end of the day, it is the family member—the son or daughter of the house who will don the mantle of leadership.

What then are the things one should look for when one is considering investing in a company as far as the management of the company is concerned?

1. To my mind the most important aspect is proven competence—their past record. How has the management managed the affairs of the company in the last three to five years? What does the record show? Has the growth been impressive or lacklustre when compared to other companies in the same industry?

2. Another point to consider is the regard or the esteem in which the management is held by its peers in the business community and in the industry. If the management is looked up to and considered worthy of emulation and adulation, the management must be capable and the judgement of the industry is usually impartial and correct.

3. The depth of knowledge of the management too must be considered—their knowledge of the industry and of the latest innovations and management techniques as it is by this that the company would be able to keep and retain its position.

4. How did the management manage at a time of adversity? Anyone can grow and make profits at a time of boom. The acid test is: Did the management manage at a time of adversity? Was it able to streamline the operations? Was it able to sell its products? Did the company perform better than its competitors? Or did the management lose control? The most capable managements prove their competence at difficult periods—under stress, strain and tension. It is at this time they prove their worth.

5. The management's integrity to the company must be beyond question. A dishonest management however capable can destroy a company by siphoning out funds or by draining the resources in diverse ways.

6. The management must be innovative. A management that does not look to the future and plan its strategy for the future is not likely to grow at the same pace as its competitors.

What then are the things one should be careful of when one considers the management of a company?

(i) It would be wise to think thrice before one invests in a company that has yet to professionalise its management. This is especially true regarding family run companies as the direction of the company's growth would be based on the whims of the head of the family and this may not be the best for the company. Decisions taken may be arrived at considering the good of the family and not the company. There may be considerable nepotism with nephews and cousins and relatives of the controlling family holding positions not on account of proven competence but due to blood ties.

(ii) It is important to determine who the major shareholders are and if they have a record of managing share prices particularly at times when they are trying to raise money from the general public through share issues, and debentures.

(iii) It would be wise to avoid investing in companies where there is infighting or where families have split. Infighting is never good for any organisation and the person who suffers most is the ordinary shareholder. In recent years a number of the more important family managed businesses have split. The period prior to the split and soon after have been periods of turbulence when performance had not been as impressive as earlier and after the split, the businesses that went to the less capable members of the family did not do well. Instances exist where companies closed down. In such situations it is always best to sit and watch from a distance. Wait until the effects of the split settle down and see how the company performs.

(iv) One of the basic principles of investment is safety. Young newer companies have a very high rate of mortality. It would be prudent to resist investing or purchasing the shares of unknown business houses or those that are yet to prove their competence.

(v) Finally one should avoid investing in companies whose management are no longer dynamic. This does happen especially in large companies which over a period of time become ponderous and bureaucratic. There are "many chiefs and few braves". They are usually top heavy and inefficient. Their performance would usually be quite revealing of its degeneration.

In India, apart from the large multinationals like Levers. Siemens and PEICO, the larger companies are family owned. However, their saving grace or rather their attraction to the common man is the fact that although at the helm they are dominated by members of the family (Tata, Birla. Singhania's etc.) the companies are managed on a day to day basis by professional managers. The controlling families too have been exposed to modern management techniques and some like Rahul Bajaj has attended prestigious educational institutions like the Harvard Business School. A family that is managing three companies well is more than likely to be managing the fourth also well.

The bottom line in determining the competence of the management is of course the "bottom line". How much has it grown over the years and in comparison to competitors. This is the real test and one should not be involved in or invest in a company in which one has doubts on the competence or integrity of its management.

16

PRICE/EARNINGS RATIO

The decision on whether a share should be bought or not is dependant on the price at which the share can be purchased. A particular company may be doing exceedingly well. Its prospects may be bright. Its management may be innovative and competent. However, if the share is very highly priced the share would not be a good purchase as an investment as the return one would get would not be as much as one may get in another—even though the other company may not be as good. In short at the time an investment decision is being made, apart from looking at the company, it is equally important to look at the price the share is priced at.

An overpriced share although it may not offer greater capital appreciation or comparatively better returns is usually a safer investment as it enjoys greater investor confidence. On the other hand under priced shares offer investment opportunities as their chances of capital appreciation are great.

What determines the price of share? How is a share priced at Rs. 20 whereas another is priced at Rs. 60. In normal circumstances what really determines the price is the investing public's confidence in the company, their belief in the future prospects of the company and its earning power (the earning the company is likely to make per share). Companies that command a better price vis-a-vis others usually have a higher earnings per share and a better earnings to equity ratio.

The price earnings ratio (P/E) is used to determine whether shares are reasonably priced—whether they should be purchased or not. It reduces to an arithmetical figure the relationship between market price and the earnings per share and by this allows investors the opportunity of making comparisons between shares.

The P/E is the most popular and the most basic of all investment indicators and the most widely used. It enables an investor to quickly determine whether a share is overpriced or underpriced. It indicates the extent the earnings per share are covered by price and an investor would thereby be able to ascertain how long it would take for him to recover his investment.

This ratio is above all a reflection of how the investing public—the market feels about the company and its ability to earn. P/E averages are available from financial newspapers and magazines for industries and companies and one can compare these with the P/E of the company one is considering investing in at the time one is considering whether to invest or not. The P/E can also reflect general opinion on the health of the economy.

The P/E ratio is calculated as follows:

$$\frac{\text{Price per Share}}{\text{Earnings per Share}}$$

The earnings per share is arrived at by dividing the profit after tax and preference dividend by the number of shares issued by the company. In short it represents the profit available to each ordinary shareholder.

Illustration

Nivya Ltd. is a public limited company engaged in the manufacture of pharmaceuticals. The company's shareholders funds at June 30, 1989 was as follows:

	Rs. 000s.
100,000 Ordinary Shares of Rs. 10 each	1,000
5,000 10% preference shares of Rs. 100 each	500
Reserves	2,500
	Rs. 4,000

The company made a profit after tax for the year ended June 30, 1989 of Rs. 750,000. The market price on August 31, 1989 was Rs. 105.

In this illustration the earnings per share of Nivya Ltd. would be—

$$\frac{\text{Profit after tax (750)} - \text{Preference dividend (50)}}{\text{Ordinary Share (100)}} = \text{Rs. 7}$$

The Price earnings ratio would be—

$$\frac{\text{Market Price 105}}{\text{Earnings Per Share (7)}} = 13$$

This translates to the submission that it would take 13 years to recoup the investment made through the earnings per share the company makes.

The P/E ratio is probably a better investment gauge than others such as the earning per share or the dividend yield as it reflects the investor opinion on the share and how the public feel about the company. Punidara Ltd. is a professionally managed multinational company involved in the manufacture of electronic gadgets. In 1988, the P/E was 15. In 1989 it fell to 12.5. This suggests, under normal conditions, that there has been a loss of confidence in the company by investors. On the other hand had the P/E risen to 18, it could mean that the investors believe that the prospects of the company would improve still further. It must of course be emphasised that this is the interpretation in normal circumstances. In a period of boom all P/Es rise as did occur in the boom of 1985. And in the depression of 1987, all P/Es fell. At these times, the fall and rise is more a reflection on how the economy is perceived by the general investing public and not the opinion of the investors on an individual company.

The question may be asked—why would a person purchase a share with a P/E of 15 or 20? The return is low and he could possibly earn much more by placing his money in a fixed deposit in a bank? The reason is that the person expects the earnings to grow at an impressive rate and if this expectation is right he stands to recover his investment much earlier than is indicated in the P/E. He therefore pays a high price because of his belief in the company and its rate of growth in the future. This is important. The price that is paid is on future prospects and earnings. In this there is a flaw in that the P/E calculation is made on the current market value and the earnings of the previous year. This can be corrected to an extent by basing the calculation on the estimated current year's and future years' earnings. This is sometimes difficult to know but one can estimate this by examining the performance of the company in the three previous years and then forecasting what its performance is likely to be in the future. In order to arrive at this one must of course consider the state of the economy, the industry the company is in and any details or information one may have heard or read about the company in the newspapers or magazines.

The P/E of a company is constantly changing and in a market that is susceptible to sharp upturns and downturns it must. The earning per share of Divya Ltd. may be Rs. 10. The market price last month may have been 100 resulting in a P/E of 10. It may be 110 today and the P/E would therefore be 11. The average investor is therefore bound to be confused. What is a fair price? What is a reasonable value for the share? Let us consider this.

The safest investment that one could possibly make is a deposit in a nationalised bank which would earn an interest of say 10%. The P/E of this is effectively 10 (Rs. 100 divided by 10%). Or one could also invest in Public bonds which pay an interest of say 15%. The P/E in this instance would be 6.6. In short for practically risk free investment the P/E is about 10.

The rewards and returns of investing in shares are greater. The risks are greater too but in view of the possibility and the chances of doubling and tripling your money in a relatively short time you should be prepared to pay more. In short shares would have a much higher P/E on account of the anticipated rewards.

On an average in a developing country like India, the average P/E of good, healthy companies is around 15. Some like Reliance (which are exceptions) are much higher. It must be remembered that one cannot say whether a high growth or a low growth company is better. What matters is the amount of the company's earning that you are prepared to pay. It is in this that one's ability to analyse comes in. If one can pick out a company that is growing fast but has a P/E of only 7 then that would be the share to buy as with growth, the price and consequently the P/E is bound to grow.

This brings one back to what P/E is reasonable. This must necessarily depend on the following—

● the rate the company's earnings are likely to grow at.
● the rate the investor expects his investments to grow.

Let us assume a share is currently priced at Rs. 20 a share and it is anticipated that it will rise to Rs. 40 in 3 years. Let us also assume that there are 2 investors, Muthu and Kuthu.

● Muthu wants to double his investment in 3 years
● Kuthu wants to triple his investment in 3 years.

In this situation Muthu would be prepared to pay Rs. 20 whereas Kuthu would not be prepared to pay more than Rs. 13.3. In short, the P/E that would be reasonable to pay would be that which fulfils your investment return require-ments based on the company's projected earnings. It would be prudent to remember though that a high P/E (over 20) can only be justified if the company is having a high growth rate—10% p.a. and over.

Prices of shares are dependent to an extent on interest rates too. When interest rates rise, people sell their shares and place their monies in interest earning deposits and securi-ties. The prices fall as demand falls. The P/E consequently falls.

A quick thumb rule in regard to deciding on whether to invest in a share or not is the 60% rule. This suggests that you should not purchase a share at a P/E that is more than 60% of the growth that you anticipate. If you felt that the earnings of Nikhila Ltd. is likely to grow by 30% p.a. you should not purchase it at a P/E that exceeds 18. At a P/E of less than 18 (assuming Nikhila Ltd. does grow at 30% p.a.) you would make a handsome profit or atleast double your money in 3 years. There are detailed tables by which one can determine, based on anticipated growth, the P/E one should pay now. As future earnings are estimates at best, the tables cannot be sworn upon as the growth in earnings may be different. The 60% rule is easier to calculate and if one bases one's decision a little cautiously one would not be too wrong.

It is difficult to predict future growth and an investor would be wise to relook at his calculations and conclusions in the light of developments as they happen. He should also remember that it is harder for a company to grow at the same percentage. A company may grow at 50% in the first year. In the second year it may be able to grow only at 40%. To sustain the same percentage as a company grows larger and yet larger is not possible.

Now, unknown and unproven companies have low P/Es and as a result may look to be attractive investments. They may be but it should be remembered that the low P/E is because the company is unknown, unproven and lacks investor confidence. Furthermore, new companies have a high mortality rate.

The P/E in short is a tremendous indicator of market sentiment, investor confidence and the earning potential of a company and a investor who purchases a share without looking at its P/E ratio does so at his peril.

17

INDUSTRY RISKS

Apart from examining the financial strengths of a company, a potential investor or lender must examine the industry within which the company operates because this could affect the very existence and survival of the company. A company's management may be superior, its balance sheet strong and its reputation enviable. However, the company may not have diversified and the industry within which it operates may be at a depression. This could result in a tremendous decline in revenues which would threaten the very continuance of the company. The shipping industry has since late 1981 been in a depression from which it has not yet fully recovered and many shipping companies have sold their ships at throwaway prices as they were not earning income and interest costs had to be reduced. Many companies had to close down too.

Many business magazines have detailed industry analysis as do financial newspapers. It would be wise to read and compare the various analysis prepared as it would give one an indication regarding the industry. If the industry is forecasted to boom it would be a worthwhile proposition to invest in the company as the likelihood of rewards are great. Similarly if the industry is projected to take a downturn, the wise man would quickly divest his investment.

What are the factors one should consider when one examines the industry within which a company operates.

1. Is it easy to enter the industry? Easy entry industries require little capital nor does it require much technological expertise. As a consequence there are a multitude of competitors. This could result eventually in intense competition resulting in very low margins and high costs.
2. Are there many competitors? If there are many and no

one competitor dominates then each of the competitors will vie with each other for a greater market share. There will be price wars and margins will reduce. A striking example of this is the T.V. market where there are many companies. Similarly there are many companies selling personal computers. Each company is trying to outdo the other and to do so are offering more to the consumer for less.

3. Is the company in a high growth industry? If the growth of this industry is over 30% p.a. persons/companies are, in the hope of earning super profits. attracted to it. The major high growth industry in recent times has been the electronics and the computer industries. The growth was over 100% initially and as a consequence many entered this industry. Another high growth industry in India in the early eighties was the leasing industry and at its high point in 1984-85 more than 200 leasing companies were floated. Now a few years later only a handful are surviving and these have diversified into other areas—to property development, to TV production and the likes.

4. Is there product differentiation? A company whose products have products differentiation has more staying power. The products of a company may be preferred because of its name or because of the quality of its products—Mercedes Benz cars or Levis Jeans or Godrej Refrigerators or Sumeet Food Processors. People are prepared to pay more for the product and consequently the products are at a premium and above competition.

5. Does the company have a fixed cost structure? If it does it would have large investments and large capital and because of this it will not have too many competitors. Its high fixed costs would have to be serviced and a fall in sales can result in a more than proportionate fall in profits. An example of such an industry is the motor industry which requires enormous capital investment. The number of companies in this industry are few and they cater to specific segments of the population.

6. What is the cost of capacity additions? If the cost of expansion is high, competitors will be few. Conse-

quently there will also be greater economies of scale.

7. What are the size of exit costs? If the costs of exit are great i.e. the payment of gratuity, unfunded provident and pension liabilities and the likes, companies would remain in the business even if the margins are low and little or no profits are being made.

8. What is the motivation of competitors? Are they in the market for prestige or for profit? If profit is not the motivating factor companies may remain in the industry even at slender margin.

9. Is there a substitute product? Can another product replace the product? The industry where this is constantly looked at is the packaging industry—beer cans replacing bottles, PVC replacing conventional paper wrapping, jute bags replacing plastic bags and so on. The list is endless.

10. How powerful are the buyers and suppliers? If they are they can force prices down or up which could be to the detriment of the industry. In scarce economies such as India, it is often the suppliers of raw materials who wield enormous power. They dictate terms, insist on payment upfront and keep to their own schedules.

11. What will be the effect of technological innovations on the product? Would it result in it becoming obsolete? An industry where great strides in technology has been made in recent years is the computer industry—with its omnis, personal computers and now it is the laptops. The things they are capable of are phenomenal and the question being asked is "now what?" and "what next?"

12. Is there great rivalry between existing competitors such as price competition and advertising wars. This can erode profits. In India we are currently in the midst of a soap war with detergent manufacturers advertising heavily and cutting prices to stay ahead of the competition. This will naturally result in lower profits as costs increase and margins decrease.

13. What is government policy? This can attract or detract competitors, it can also result in higher or lower profits. This is why every industry waits anxiously in February for the budget because it is this that will largely deter-

mine the company's results in the next year.

14. Are there international cartels? In the coffee industry, the supply far exceeds the demand. In order to protect against widely fluctuating prices, the international coffee organisation which is made up of coffee exporting and importing countries have fixed the price of a bag of coffee and the quantity that a country may export. In such situations a coffee exporting company is ensured of a sale and a definite price (which would result in a certain profit.

While examining and studying the industry in which a company operates, it is important to also study demand for the products of the industry and of the company in particular. The items one should consider when assessing demand are:—

(a) Is the business in a high growth industry and if so, can management operate at a high level? Low growth can be alright as the business may be able then to finance its activity with internally generated funds?

(b) How essential is the product or is it just a fad?

(c) Is the demand predictable? In the food industry demand is predictable whereas it is not so in the refrigerator industry.

(d) Is the business volatile. Usually highly financial businesses are very volatile.

(e) Is demand cyclical. Demand may be only at periods.

(f) What would happen to the product demand if a structural change takes place in the economy? In 1973 the Opec Cartel affected many industries.

(g) What will be the effect on demand if a change in government policy takes place? A high tax on imports can stimulate demand for domestic products. Similarly if the government reduces import duty on certain articles, demand can shift to imported items.

(h) How will exchange fluctuations affect demand. In 1984 the dollar strengthened and this cut the costs of imports into the United Kingdom and stimulated consumer demand. Similarly the weakening of the rupee has made Indian articles more cost attractive abroad.

Another factor which is important is that all industries have cycles which is often compared to a day. The initial period is known as the sun rise. This is a period of growth and the growth is usually quite remarkable. It apexes at noon. At this time there are many competitors and the industry is maturing. Upto this period, it is good to enter the industry as the profits make it more than worthwhile. There is a period of consolidation which can be for some time. Eventually things change, demand falls and noon becomes evening, then dusk and finally sunset. Investing in a sunset industry is shortsighted as the investment is likely to turn sour.

It is imperative therefore that at the time a company is being considered as an investment that the industry, the company is operating in is considered as this will determine whether the investment will be profitable or not.

18

CROSS COUNTRY EXPOSURE

Citibank, in 1987 provided for more than a billion dollars for losses in South America. Bank of America and many other American banks have suffered enormous losses in Latin American Loans. The reason was that the countries in Latin America were unable to pay for the loans they had received. A similar problem exists in Africa too—in countries like Nigeria that have severe balance of payments problems. An Indian company had a few years ago exported to a Nigerian company certain machines. The importing company paid the money to the bank. There it   still lies. It could not be sent to the importer as the Central Bank of the country refused the foreign exchange to make the payment.

The message is clear. Whenever a person is examining the annual report of a company he should also study the country in which it operates and if it is dependent on another country for its imports or exports, the stability of that other country. The areas that should be considered are:—

1. **The political stability of the country**

The political stability of a country is of paramount impo tance. No industry or company can survive or grow in a country in political turmoil. In disturbed times there is great uncertainty. Survival is a day to day affair and dependant not on industry but on the benevolence of those in power. A company could prosper one day and be in the doldrums in the next. An ideal example that comes to mind is Sri Lanka a beautiful island which was thriving as an exporter of tea; a tourist's paradise and a producer of pearls and precious stones. This country is now at civil war and the economy is an absolute mess. No industry or company can thrive in such an environment.

2. **The rate of inflation**

Inflation has an enormous effect. If the rate of inflation in the country from which one imports is high, then the cost of production will automatically go up. This might reduce the cost competitiveness of the product finally manufactured. Conversely if the rate of inflation in the country to which one exports is high, the products manufactured would become more attractive resulting in increased sales. The South American countries suffer inflation at over 100% p.a. (in some countries it is as high as 1000% p.a.). Money has no real value. However, exports from South America is attractive purely because on account of their galloping inflation and consequent devaluation of their currency, their products are cheaper.

3. Foreign exchange risk

This is real risk and one must be cognizant of the effect of a revaluation or devaluation of the currency either in the home country or in the country the company deals with. A devaluation in the home country would make the products the company makes more attractive in other countries. It would also make imports more expensive which could have an adverse effect to sales. A devaluation in the country to which the company exports would make the company's products more expensive. In order to hedge against a devaluation in the country in which one operates, most importing companies enter into a forward foreign exchange contract thereby crystallising the amount of the liability and ensuring that the company would not be exposed to an unexpected loss should a devaluation occur.

4. Nationalisation

This is a real threat in many countries—the fear that a company may become nationalised. Historically (with very few exceptions), nationalised companies are less efficient than their private sector counterparts. If one is dependant on a company for certain supplies, nationalisation could result in supplies becoming erratic and the likes.

5. Restrictive practices

Restrictive practices or cartels imposed by countries can have, depending on the company's needs a tremendous effect on its imports or exports. The USA has restrictions regarding the imports of a variety of articles like textiles etc. Licences are given and amounts that may be imported from companies/countries are clearly detailed. India has a number of restrictions on what may be imported and at what rate of duty. This, to an extent, determines the price at which the goods can be sold. If the domestic industry is to be supported, the duties levied may be increased resulting in imports becoming unattractive. If certain industries like the electronic industry are to be encouraged, duties would be reduced as has been done recently.

It is therefore important when viewing a company to see how sensitive it is to governmental policies and the extent changes can affect the company.

6. Economic/business cycle.

Economic/business cycles in a country can drastically affect the performance of a company. If a country is going through a recession companies flounder whereas in a boom they prosper.

- recession
- recovery
- boom.

During a period of recession, demand is low and sales are low. Companies at this time often suffer a large fall in profits and even losses. Conversely at a period of recovery or boom consumer demand is high, sales are on the increase and so are profits.

While analysing a company operating in another country one should determine—

- the stage of the economic/business cycle.
- the expected duration of the cycle
- the company's ability to survive as demonstrated previously to weather recession
- at what stage of the cycle the company is likely to be most affected.

It is important to remember that losses are always at a time when accelerating inflation is followed by recession. There is, however, nothing to suggest that a boom or a recession would be for a definite period of time and hence the length of previous cycles should not be used as a measure to fore-cast the length of an existing cycle.

A manner in which a company can hedge the risk of monies not being received when it sells its goods is to insist on receiving irrevocable letters of credit opened by banks located in countries that do not have foreign exchange problems. This is easily possible. If goods are to be sold to Nigeria one should insist on receiving a letter of credit opened by a bank in London or Germany. This will ensure the receipt of sale proceeds. Problems will arise however if a company is dependant on another country for its imports. The political environment may change; the currency may be revalued; a whole host of things may occur which may affect production, sales and ultimately profits.

It is vital therefore while analysing a company that one examines and studies its exposure and dependance to companies in other countries.

159

19

HUMAN RESOURCE ACCOUNTING

The last decade has been an exciting one for men of finance. New concepts have been considered, ideas discussed, principles applied and beliefs argued. The result has been the discarding of victorian ideas and ideals and the accounting profession has hurled itself into the twentieth century and made accountancy today an exact and one of the most modern and logical of sciences.

The most revolutionary concepts in accountancy today is Human Resource Accounting—the idea that persons employed by a company should be valued and the value of these persons should be included among the assets in the Balance Sheet. The suggestion is based on the belief that the persons who make the company are responsible for the growth, profitability and viability of the company. It is argued that a company understates its assets if the value of good personnel is not reflected in its financial statements and that it overvalues its net worth if the liability created by bad management is not evaluated. Companies in which it is imperative that the value of human resources are accounted for are professional firms and service industries. Their growth and very existence depends on the ability and capability of their personnel.

Under conventional historical cost accounting the costs incurred on employees are written off in the year it is spent as revenue expenditure. The basis for this is that the company is contractually bound to pay a certain amount to employees and costs of employment must therefore be charged to the period it is incurred. As employees are not owned by the company and are free to leave the expenditure incurred as wages etc. should be immediately expensed. It would have been different had there been slaves. Slaves would have been owned assets with an useful life and like other fixed assets would have been capitalised and written off over its useful life.

When a company is purchased or valued, the value arrived at is usually higher than the net realisable value of the company's assets. The difference between the market value and the net realisable value of the assets is known in common parlance as goodwill—the value placed on the reputation of the company. The major component of this is, though it is not usually acknowledged, the value placed on the employees and the management of the company.

Human resource is an important factor of production and its valuation is therefore imperative. This is what human resource accounting attempts to do.

Let us now examine its definitions and the methods human resources can be accounted.

Definitions

The American Accounting Association's Committee on Human Resources Accounting defines Human Resource (Asset) Accounting as "the process of identifying and measuring data about human resources and communicating this information to interested parties. Davidson expands this in Accounting: the language of business as "A term used to describe and emphasise the importance of human resources—knowledgeable, trained and loyal employees—in a company's earning process and total assets." The company that was among the pioneers of human resource accounting was R.G. Barry Corporation and they define it in a more practical way. This company defines it as an attempt to identify and report investment made in human resources of an organisation that are presently not accounted for under conventional accounting practices.

In short human resources or asset accounting attempts to place a value on the people the company employs to the organisation in an attempt to show their importance to the company and to differentiate it from other similar companies. There may be two companies of a similar size in an industry. One may be old and well established employing extremely competent and diligent people. Another company

161

may not be having employees as well qualified. The value of the human resources and thus the intrinsic value of the former company would be higher. This is what human resource accounting attempts to do. Service industries and professional firms depend entirely on their personnel for their growth and even for their very survival. Human resource accounting measures the value of these personnel to the organisation and by this clearly identifies the ones that have more experienced and more competent staff.

Extract of a Balance Sheet:

DIVYA LIMITED

	(in Rs. lakhs)	
	1988	1989
Investment in Human Resources	11317	11736

Extract of Schedule in the Financial Report:

DIVYA LIMITED

	(in Rs. lakhs)	
	1988	1989
Directors & Senior Management	426	442
Managerial Staff	1238	1541
Executives	1931	2054
Supervisory & Clerical	2258	2061
Labour	5464	5638
	11317	11736

Methods of Valuation

Now that it is agreed that there is a logic and reason for human resources accounting how is it to be measured. How do you value a human being and place a value on him as an individual or to the organisation. In the days of slavery this was comparatively easy. The value of a slave was what it cost to purchase him or to acquire a similar one from the market place. Those days are gone now. It is the age of democracy and freemen today. So how then are human resources to be valued ?

The methods by which human resources are currently accounted for are as follows :—

1. *Capitalisation of historical costs:* This is a method deve
loped by R. Likert of R.G. Barry Corporation. This is the only
method which uses financial data and presents it as an asset
in the financial statements. It involves the capitalisation of all
costs of recruiting, hiring, training, development and all
other initial costs. The amount so capitalised is written off
over the period an employee remains with the organisation.
If he leaves before the period anticipated the amount
remaining as an asset is written off in its entirety.

Illustration

Nikhila Ltd. hired Anand as a trainee. The company spent
Rs. 10,000 on advertisements to hire him. Anand was sent on
numerous courses and intensive training programmes.
These cost Rs. 90,000/-. The value of Mr. Anand as a human
resource to the company is Rs. 100,000. Anand is expected
to be with the company for 20 years and hence Rs. 5000
would be written off every year. If Anand is offered a more
responsible position by Divya Ltd. four years later and moves
on there would be Rs. 80,000 that is yet to be written off. In
the fifth year the entire Rs. 80,000/- would be written off.

The major attraction of this method is that is easy to
compute but it is hardly reflective of the real value of human
resources. Training and recruiting costs alone cannot determine the value of a resource. A very competent manager
may be hired from an organisation with no real recruitment
costs. Under this method he would have no value whereas
the trainee cited in the example above who makes no mea-
sureable contribution to the organisation has a value of
Rs. 1,00,000/-. Obviously the values are not right. Hence,
under this method the value arrived at is not the real value of
human resources nor does it really indicate the contribution
made by the employees or the value of the employees to the
organisation. It is therefore of no real value to any one
reading the financial statements of a company.

2. *The Replacement Cost Method:* The Replacement cost
method, first propounded by Flamholfz in 1973, suggests
two methods i.e. individual replacement costs (IRC) and
positional replacement costs (PRC). IRC refers to the costs

that would be incurred to replace an individual with another who is capable of and able to do all the services the individual being replaced has been able to do. In short this is the value of an employee to the firm. PRC on the other hand is the cost of replacing an individual who occupies a certain position i.e. a sales manager or a factory manager. It is the value the organisation places on a particular position and therein lies its weakness—in that the value is subjective. In two similar concerns the value placed for a position would be different as the importance given would vary.

On account of the wide variations in value that can be arrived at under this method this is of no real value.

3. *Opportunity Cost Method:* This method which owes its origin to Hekiman and Jones is based on opportunity cost. It suggests that the value of an employee in an alternative use should be the basis for estimating the value of the human resource. The opportunity cost value could be established by competitive bidding within the company and the amount bid is the value of the employee. If employees are plentiful and there is no scarcity managers may not bid for employees. In such situations under this method employees have no value. A human asset has a value only if it is a scarce resource and when its employment in one division derives the services of the employee to another division.

The major deficiency of this method is that it suggests that employees that can be hired easily have no value. It claims that only those resources that are scarce have a value. This is not correct.

4. *Economic value method:* Human Resources are valued, under the economic value method, on the basis of the present value of the contribution that is likely to be made by the employees to the organisation during the period of their employment. The value thus arrived at is to be shown as a fixed asset on the face of the Balance Sheet.

As it is practically impossible to estimate the contribution made by an employee in terms of sales made or fees earned, this method suggests that the remuneration to be paid to an employee during his employment be estimated and discounted by an appropriate amount to arrive at an estimated present value. The total thus arrived at for all employees is the value of human assets employed by the company.

Although this is among the more acceptable method the major criticism is that no company pays an employee an amount equal to the benefits it derives from that employee's service. Additionally earnings etc. are earned collectively by persons working as a team and not by single individuals. Whereas the sales made by a salesman can be accurately determined, it is impossible to calculate the benefits derived from a factory worker or an administration officer or an accountant. It is also argued that capitalisation of future expenses is not really correct. What should be shown as the value is the benefit expected to accrue and not the likely expense that is to be incurred in the future.

5. *Discounted salary and wages:* This method, first propounded by Lev & Schwartz, involves determining the value of human resources as the estimated future earnings which the employees will earn upto the time they retire and then discounting this by the cost of capital. The purpose of this is to suggest that the performance of an organisation should reflect on its human resources value also. If this is not done a company that pays very high salaries would appear to have a high human asset figure and this may not be indicative of the company's performance.

Under this method, salaries are used as the base for the value of human resources. The error here is that employees are not paid in relation to their value to the organisation. It is also assumed the employee would remain in the same position till he retires. This is unlikely. These will be promotions. He may leave. His position may become, on account of technological progress, redundant.

This approach however has been the most popular in India and has been followed by notable companies such as BHEL & SAIL who have attempted to place a value to their human resources.

Human resource accounting is without a doubt an exciting concept and its wide use would enable investors, creditors and the general public to evaluate the potential of a company more accurately. The present deterrent to its wide usage is the lack of a totally acceptable method of arriving at the value of human resources.

PART IV

SELECTED ACCOUNTING TERMINOLOGY

Accelerated depreciation — A method where the depreciation charge becomes progressevely smaller each period.

Accounts payable — This is a liability and represents an amount owed to a creditor usually arising from the purchase of raw materials, stores and supplies. This is also known as "trade creditors".

Accounts receivable — This is an asset and represents amounts due from customers arising from sales or services rendered. This is also terms as "trade debtors".

Accounting changes — This is defined as a change in the accounting principle of calculating values etc. such as the change in the method of valuation of stock from first in first out to last in first out.

Accounting errors arithmetic — Errors and misapplications of accounting principles in previously published Accounts that are corrected in the period under review—the adjustment being done to the balance on the profit and loss account.

Accounting policies — The accounting principles that have been adopted by the company.

Accretion — This is defined as the increase in value of an asset through a physical change (increase in value of a plantation caused by the plants growing).

Affiliated company — A company controlling or controlled by another company.

Advances to affiliates — Loans by holding company to a subsidiary or affiliate company.

Application of funds — Any transaction that reduces funds.

Appraisal — The valuation by an expert of an asset or a liability.

Appropriation — An amount of after tax profits set aside for a specific purpose.

Bad debt — An amount due that is uncollectible.

Bonus shares — Shares given to shareholders in proportion to their holding without a capital outflow from the shareholder.

Book value — The value of an asset in the books of account. This is also known as written down value.

Capital expenditure — Expenditure incurred to acquire long term assets.

Cash discount — A reduction in sales or purchase price due to prompt payment.

Cash flow — Cash receipts less cash payments.

Contingent Liability — A liability that would arise should an event occur such as a bill discounted being dishonoured by the drawer.

Creditor — One who is owed money

Debt — An amount owed

Debtor — One who borrows

Disclosure — The stating of facts in the Accounts

Dividend — An amount paid to shareholders from profits earned by the company.

Earned surplus — This is another term for the balance on the profit and loss account.

Extraordinary item — An income or expense of an unusual nature.

Fair Market Value — The price that the item is valued at in an open market.

Finished goods — Manufactured goods ready for sale.

Forward exchange contract — An agreement to either purchase or sell foreign exchange at a specified price in the future.

Goodwill — The excess of cost of a company acquired over the fair market value of the net assets of the company.

Gross — Not adjusted or reduced by deduction.

Guarantee — A promise to answer for payment of a debt in the event of an occurrence.

Hidden reserve — This relates to the understatement of the shareholders' funds. This arises by the undervaluation of assets or overvaluation of liabilities.

Holding company — A company whose activities consist of owning shares in and controlling the management of other companies.

Holding gain or loss — Difference between the end of period price and beginning of period price of an asset.

Hypothecation — The pledging of property without transfer of title or possession, to secure a loan.

Indeterminate-term liabilities — A liability not meeting the criterion of being due at a definite time.

Inflation accounting — A method of accounting to show the effect of the fall in the purchasing power of the currency-the proper name for this is current cost accounting.

Intangible asset — A nonphysical, noncurrent right that gives a company a benefit or an expense the benefit from which may be received over a period of time.

Inventory-Stock — Goods the company sells or uses to manufacture its products.

Invested capital — Amount contributed by shareholders.

Issued shares — Number of shares issued.

Kiting — The illegal or wrongful use of float for personal purposes.

Know how — Business or technical information that is an expertise and knowledge developed through experience.

Lapping — Theft by an employee of cash sent in by a customer to discharge his debts.

Lead time — The time that it takes between the placing of an order and the receipt of the goods.

Lien — A charge on an asset of the borrower by the lender.

Limited liability — Shareholders' liability in a company is limited only to amount not paid on shares allotted to them. He is not liable on the company's debts.

Line of credit — An agreement with a bank whereby the bank gives credit facilities for shortterm borrowings including overdrafts.

Liquidation — Payment of a debt or closing down of a business.

Liquidity — Availability of cash or cash equivalents to pay liabilities.

Market rate — Rate of interest a company would need to pay to borrow funds.

Materiality — The opinion that only those events or details that are important should be mentioned for understanding the accounts.

Merger — The joining of two companies into a single entity.

Minority interest — The interest of the small shareholders who are not part of the controlling shareholders.

Mortgage — A change given by the borrower to secure a loan.

Negotiable — Legally capable of being transferred by endorsement like bills of exchange.

Net — Reduced by all relevant deductions.

Net sales — Sales less returns, discounts and freight paid for customers.

Net realisable value — The sales price less expenses to mak the item ready to sell.

Nonrecurring — An event that is unlikely to happen again and again.

Obsolescence — Decline in market value of an asset caused by better and more efficient alternatives becoming available.

Opportunity cost — The income that could be or could have been earned if the asset had been used in the best way.

172

Overdraft — A short term given for working capital purposes.

Paper profit — An unrealised gain.

Par — Face value

Parent company — The company owning 50% of the share capital and controls it.

Pledging — The borrower assigns assets as security or collateral for the repayment of a loan.

Plough back — The retaining of assets generated by earnings for continued investment in the business.

Post statement-events — Events happening after the date of the Balance Sheet that could have a very major effect on the company.

Premium — The excess of issue price over the face value of a share.

Prepayment — Payments made for future benefits.

Present value — Value to-day of an amount to be paid or received at a future date calculated taking into account an acceptable discount rate.

Promissory note — An unconditional promise in writing to pay a specified sum of money on demand or at a specified date.

Prorate — Allocate in proportion to a base.

Provision — An amount set aside from profits for an estimated loss.

Proxy written — Authority given by a shareholder to another to vote on his behalf.

Qualified report — An Auditor's report wherein the auditor states he is not happy with the treatment of one or more items as a consequence of which he has doubts.

Redemption — Retirement by the company of debentures and bonds

Reserve — An appropriation of profit.

Revenue expenditure — An expense.

173

Rights — The privilege or right to subscribe for new shares.

Secret reserve — Hidden reserve.

Sight draft — A demand for payment addressed to the borrower.

Sound value — Fair or market value

Subsidiary — A company which is owned by another or one where another company owns more that 50% of the share capital.

Taking a bath — To incur a large loss

Tax shield — The amount of an expense that reduces taxable income but does not require working capital.

Trade acceptance — A draft drawn by a seller which is presented for signatures (acceptance) to the buyer at the time goods are purchased.

Trade credit — Time given for the purchaser/customer to pay.

Trade-in — Acquisition of new asset in exchange (partly or wholly) for another asset.

Uncollectible item — An amount receivable from the debtor that will not be paid.

Unearned Income — Advances received for which the work is not completed.

Variance — Difference between actual and standard cost of income or expense.

Working asset — A natural reserve having a limited useful life.

Window dressing — An attempt to make financial statements show operating results or financial position more favourable than would be otherwise.

Write off — Charge an asset to expense or loss.

Zero salvage value — The value of an asset being nil at the time of damage or end of useful life.